WHAT OTHERS ARE SAYING—

On first glance, Todd Starnes has penned a witty look at his journey regarding his struggle with food and personal health issues. But this humorous and well-written book is much more than a self-portrait of Todd's autobiographical journey. In these pages the reader will be called afresh to think about what is involved in being and becoming a faithful follower of Jesus Christ. Readers will certainly laugh and empathize with the way Todd describes his background and personal struggles, but moreover, readers will be asked to reconsider their own choices in all areas of life. I am sure that this book will be an encouragement to many.

—David S. Dockery
President
Union University

It's been said truth is stranger than fiction, and Todd Starnes' book illustrates perfectly that humor is found in the everyday realities of life. From the family supper table to the streets of New York—through personal tragedy and triumph—this talented storyteller leaves readers of all ages wanting to learn more.

I laughed, I cried, but mostly, I could relate—though I'm not a man, I'm not a runner, I haven't ever lived in New York, I don't eat pork rinds, and I haven't had heart surgery. On the other hand, I've lost a parent, I do care about interfaith relations, I struggle with weight issues, and I love Jesus Christ and daily experience His grace and mercy in my life. Readers will find something with which they can relate, whatever their experience.

Todd takes those who won't be able to put down the book with him on a vivid journey where he reaches to the bottom of his soul for answers. And when he comes up chuckling through it all, the readers, through both smiles and tears, will have connected in a profound way with a storyteller who has found his voice.

—Joni B. Hannigan
Managing Editor
Florida Baptist Witness

Todd Starnes is an accomplished journalist and the ultimate professional, but he has peeled away the formalities of news reporting to share his personal experience in how God gently dispenses His tender mercies. His story is personal and sometimes Southern homespun, but not contrived. He doesn't dish out ideology, but he deals with some of the big ideas about God in a way that is real and fun and compelling to read.

—Will Hall
Executive Editor
Baptist Press

Todd Starnes' stories will make you laugh, touch your heart, and encourage you to take steps toward living a better life. Todd's story reminds me of the many ups and downs I faced during my weight loss. Along his journey Todd not only lost a significant amount of weight, but he also lost his parents to sudden illnesses. He survived a significant surgery, ran a marathon, and despite it all still managed to complete the task. Todd's story reminds us that God uses the least of us to do the greatest things, that way there is no question that it is indeed God at work. Todd's story is an honest story told with a healthy dose of humor. This book fits the prescription for whatever ails you. Laughter really is the best medicine. When we find ourselves at our weakest point, that is when our true strength is revealed. I hope you will be inspired after reading this book. I know I was.

—Mike Huckabee
Former Arkansas Governor

All of us have a story—amazing and intimate stories, ups and downs, mountaintops and valleys, laughter and tears, victories and heartaches, good days and bad days, healthy days and sick days, wins and losses, and seasons, so many seasons of life, all adding up to your special story, your adventure.

Rarely do we get to go behind the curtain of one's life to experience the intimacy of the journey. Todd Starnes invites us to join him in his journey of life, his seasons of pain, hurt, victory, and change. He gives us a glimpse of those days when God came crashing into the deepest parts of his heart and mind.

I have no doubt you will find yourself somewhere in Todd's story and say, "Wow, that's me!" Perhaps it will be a childhood with a loving mom and dad and family. Or perhaps it's learning to love food that is so tasty and so bad for you. Maybe it is the doctor who says you have a problem, a disease, a crisis, a need to change or you might die soon. Or maybe it's sorting out what your life's purpose is.

Welcome to Todd's world: vulnerability, laughter, heartache, disappointment, career changes, an unhealthy lifestyle, a very sick heart, tough words from a doctor, a road to change and recovery, a road to the finish line at the New York City Marathon, a strong family foundation, and a relentless love for barbecue. Some things a man simply can't go without.

Todd Starnes is a brilliant communicator. He speaks from his heart to yours. And he speaks with transparency and intimacy. With God guiding his heart and mind, Todd continues to write his story. Thankfully, Todd has stopped long enough to share what has been written so far—and to give you a glimpse into his dreams for the next season of life.

—Don Boykin
Deputy Managing Editor (retired)
Atlanta Journal Constitution

Todd Starnes is heard by many thousands each day on Fox News Radio, but I can assure you that the story you are about to "hear" him tell is one that is more inspiring than any you will hear on the radio. Todd's words are sure to make you laugh, make you cry, and help you understand the incredible truths of the human experience when God is part of your journey. This is a book you will want to read more than once!

—Jonathan Falwell
Pastor
Thomas Road Baptist Church

This book has a very catchy title, but wait until you hear my friend Todd Starnes' story. Meet the man with the great big heart from the family that prays about butter. It's about how the love of food can kill you and how to step away from the cheesecake.

—Steve Doocy
Host
Fox & Friends

It's not often you find a book that makes your face hurt while reading it, but when you smile for hours on end, it makes sense. Todd hits the mark in this true-life story that is funny, poignant, and most of all, spiritually uplifting. It's a rare combination, but when you pop the hood open on this book, you don't just find gravy on the dipstick. You find a must-read pleasure!

—David Brody
Senior Political Correspondent
Christian Broadcasting Network

Todd Starnes was, by his own definition, a three-hundred-pound guy with a bad heart. Already a professing believer in Christ, Todd's open-heart surgery forced him to reevaluate his priorities. Literally given a second chance at life, he reduced his weight to a mere one hundred fifty pounds and became a marathon runner. Today, Todd lives an active, healthier life in New York City as a network news reporter and anchor for Fox News Radio.

During his marathon of weight loss, Todd not only lost one hundred fifty pounds of excess weight, he lost both of his parents to sudden illnesses. This book is his story. Relax! It is not a story about weight loss, although he does tell about that in the book. This is a well-written, more-often-than-not humorous, yet sobering look at life. Get ready to hold your stomach as you laugh out loud, only to reach for your handkerchief as you fight back the tears.

—James E. Cossey
Editor in Chief
Pathway Press

THEY POPPED MY HOOD AND FOUND GRAVY ON THE DIPSTICK

TODD STARNES

FOREWORD BY MIKE HUCKABEE

THEY POPPED MY HOOD AND FOUND GRAVY ON THE DIPSTICK

PATHWAY PRESS

Scripture quotations are taken from the *New King James Version*.
Copyright © 1979, 1980, 1982, 1990, 1995, Thomas Nelson Inc.,
Publishers.

This book is based on fact, but some elements are fictionalized.

Editorial Staff: James E. Cossey, Tom George, Tammy Hatfield,
and Jessica Tressler.

Cover Design by Wayne Slocumb
Interior Design by Tom George

Library of Congress Catalog Card Number: 2009921043
ISBN: 978-1-59684-436-0

Copyright © 2009 by Pathway Press
1080 Montgomery Avenue
Cleveland, Tennessee 37311

Visit www.pathwaypress.org for more information.

Printed in the United States of America

For

Michael Winn

and

Cory Gearrin

CONTENTS

ACKNOWLEDGMENTS

I've met so many wonderful people along this journey, and to mention them all would require another book. But there are some special individuals without whom this book would not have been written. My parents, Jim and Kathy Starnes, have already reached their journey's end. I miss them more than you can imagine. Dad taught me to love Christ and Mom taught me to read. Both lessons have served me well.

My grandmother, Billie Starnes, has played a significant role in my life. Her wisdom and her prayers have guided every step I've made. And so has my Aunt Lynn. She inspired me to read at an early age. Whenever she came to visit our home, she would always give me a few of her books by Erma Bombeck and Fannie Flagg. I was probably the only kid in my junior high school who could quote from Bombeck's *If Life Is a Bowl of Cherries, What Am I Doing in the Pits?*

I am also thankful for my cousin Billy. He committed to being my prayer partner through the writing of this book, and his intercession is one of the reasons this book is being published.

I'm blessed to have a great family scattered from Traveler's Rest, South Carolina, to Tacoma, Washington. All of them were involved in this process—poking, prodding, and encouraging me along the way: the aunts and uncles, Bob and Sue, Jerry and Lynn, Bill and Sue, Joe and Barb; my brother, Robert; the cousins, Amy and Lance, Clint and Shala, Jeff and Saundra, Andy and Caroline, Billy, Jen, Kristina (yes, I really did finish the book, Kristina) and Thomas (who has me wrapped around his finger), Taylor, Hannah, Luke, Seth, Daniel, David, Dylan, Lauren, Kyle, Caden; Aunt Hazel and Uncle Bunny—my biggest fans; and Uncle Gene and Aunt Bodil.

I'm especially grateful to the guys—Andy Botts, David Hicks, Michael Winn, and Cory Gearrin. Whether we were hiking through Yosemite or white-water rafting, you kept things exciting!

I've been especially thankful to know Don and Lynn Boykin. Don is a spiritual giant and one of the finest newspapermen I know. Lynn and I developed a special bond through our mutual heart ailments.

To Kevin Sajdak, I'm thankful for the extra set of eyes on this project as well as our dinnertime debates.

To Blake Henry, there just aren't enough words. Your friendship has made this city a nicer place to live.

To Sarah Haley, you know how to shoot a gun and cook a casserole. But most importantly, you make me smile.

I'm grateful to my colleagues at KFBK in Sacramento, especially Judy Farah, Marianne Russ, Kitty O'Neal, Lori Lundin, Laura Podolak, Tom Sullivan, Sheldon Orvis, Ken Kohl, and Alan Eisenson.

I also want to thank my colleagues at Fox News in New York, among them Roger Ailes, Kevin Magee, Bob Finnerty, Mich Davis, Dianne Brandi, Kristen Hess, Hank Weinbloom, Steve Doocy, Lauren Green, and Valerie Alexander. What a blessing it's been to work with such fine professionals. I've been so honored to practice journalism with you.

I'm especially thankful to Dawn Weiner, a fellow Southerner and my colleague at Fox News Radio. She was such an encouragement as I started running and organized a group to run alongside me at my very first road race. Her kindness was such a blessing.

Also, I am thankful to Fox News Radio's Website Wizard—Willie Sanchez—for teaching me to blog and twitter.

To my church family at First Baptist Fair Oaks, you people are so dear to me. Pastor J. T. and Brenda Reed, Wayne and Nancy, Bob and Shirley, Tom and Jeannine, Teri and Jim, you represent the best in a New Testament congregation. I love you all.

There are many others to acknowledge including Dr. David Dockery; Jim and Carol Veneman; Morris and Sandy Abernathy; Arnold and Vickie Botts; Scott and Robin Hicks; Alan and Teresa Rosenhauer; Ed and Susan Winn; John and Cindy Cook; Geri Gearrin; Will Hall; Art Toalston; Tammy Rosson; Joni Hannigan; Robyn Walensky; Anderson McGregor; Kellen Distefano, who taught me to step out of my comfort zone; Nelson Searcy and Kerrick Thomas, my pastors at The Journey Church; the staff of the Starbucks on Seventh Avenue in Brooklyn, where I wrote this book—you guys kept my coffee cup filled.

To the staff at Sutter Memorial Hospital, the nurses on the fourth floor, and the doctors at Sacramento Heart, thank you for saving my life.

And, of course, I appreciate the wonderful team at Pathway Press—Joseph Mirkovich, general director of publications, and my editors, James E. Cossey and Tom George.

And most of all, to the Author of my salvation—my Lord and Savior, Jesus Christ, who gave me life everlasting—my constant companion on this never-ending journey.

FOREWORD

Every journey needs to start somewhere, and Todd's, like mine, started because of a talk with a doctor.

I can identify with Todd. Like most kids growing up in the South, I was raised to believe that the only way of cooking anything was to first batter it in cornmeal or flour and then fry every last bit of nutrition out of it in a pan of scalding-hot grease. For most of my life I was sustained on fried food and all I was doing was digging my own grave with a knife and a fork. We should all remember that we need to eat to live, but we should not live to eat.

One step at a time is how Todd Starnes began his physical comeback. One step at a time is how we all should live our lives. It is never easy to take steps to change your lifestyle. And, as you will discover in this book, Todd was not convinced he could make the changes his body demanded of him, but he found the courage by doing it one step at a time.

Todd's stories will make you laugh, touch your heart, and encourage you to take steps toward living a better life. Todd's story reminds me of the many ups and downs I faced during my weight loss. Along his journey, Todd not only lost a significant amount of weight, but he also lost his parents to sudden illnesses. He survived a significant surgery, ran a marathon, and, despite it all, still managed to complete the task. Todd's story reminds us that God uses the least of us to do the greatest things. That way there is no question that it is indeed God at work.

Todd's story is an honest story—told with a healthy dose of humor. This book fits the prescription for whatever ails you. Laughter really is the best medicine. When we find ourselves at our weakest point, that is when our true strength is revealed.

I hope you will be inspired after reading this book. I know I was.

—Mike Huckabee
Former Arkansas Governor

INTRODUCTION

"Todd, if you don't have this surgery, you will die."

It was a warm spring day in May 2005. I was a news reporter for KFBK in Sacramento, California—the place where Rush Limbaugh got his big break and where I hoped to get mine. I loved my job and the people I worked with. We were a motley crew, but all of us had a passion for journalism. And when word of a hostage standoff filtered into the newsroom, I bolted out the door. It was a normal, run-of-the-mill standoff—at a seedy motel just off the interstate. But it was during our coverage that I developed a slight cough.

A few days later I could barely get out of bed. I was terribly exhausted. I just chalked it up to weighing three hundred pounds (I had a hard time turning down all-you-can-eat buffets). The cough got progressively worse. *Must be allergies*, I thought. By the end of the week, I was coughing up lunch, dinner, and what appeared to be my spleen (as you will soon discover, I do relish hyperbole). I figured it was time to get checked out.

It took one X-ray to discover the source of my problem, and it wasn't allergies. My heart was beginning to fail. As I will explain later in this book, my aortic valve was shot—thanks to a genetic quirk. And there was only one way to fix the problem.

"Yes, you need heart surgery," said the doctor.

I was stunned. Going to see the doctor is sort of like buying a car. You go into the dealership expecting to buy a sensible, affordable vehicle and you leave in a shiny red convertible. One minute I had bronchitis, and the next thing I knew, this surgeon wanted to pry me open with a crowbar and fiddle around with my insides.

But the doctor was quite serious. I was lucky to be alive, he said. And without the surgery, he told me death was not just a possibility—it was a certainty.

I fumbled around with my day planner and told him I could fit in the surgery sometime in early July. And that's when he leveled the bombshell. "Todd, if you don't have this surgery, you will die." He gave me two weeks to get my affairs in order.

And that's how it all began—on a warm spring day, in a heart surgeon's office in Sacramento.

God, it seemed, had been trying to get my attention. And I wasn't listening. You know, there are some folks that just need a nudge from the Lord. Others need to be poked and prodded into following His call. Then there are believers like me, who require a bit more severe persuasion— like ripping open your chest and whacking your heart.

One of the littlest ones in our family tried to get a handle on my predicament.

"Cousin Todd, will they see Jesus when they open your heart?"

What a profound question—and one that I've pondered through this long, difficult, and most wonderful journey. Honestly, there were some days when the answer was no. People did not see Jesus in my life. The laundry list of excuses was, of course, inexcusable—like the time I used my heart condition to get out of Vacation Bible School duties. Ouch!

My story is not unique. Many people have survived open-heart surgery. Many people have lost weight. And many people have lost their parents. Nevertheless, this is *my* story.

So how did I do it? How does a three-hundred-pound guy with a bad heart survive major surgery, lose one hundred fifty pounds, and run the New York City Marathon? Since I don't normally sleep in a Holiday Inn Express, I can't allow them to take credit. Friends, this was truly a Holy Spirit moment! The Scriptures tell us that God's mercies are new every morning, and they certainly are. He has given me a measure of grace to survive the bad days and treasure the good ones. And I learned that when life seemed to spiral out of control, God was still *in* control.

A prophet in the Old Testament understood what I was about to go through. Habakkuk penned a hymn of faith:

> Though the fig tree may not blossom,
> Nor fruit be on the vines;
> Though the labor of the olive may fail,

And the fields yield no food;
Though the flock may be cut off from the fold,
And there be no herd in the stalls—
Yet I will rejoice in the Lord,
I will joy in the God of my salvation.
The Lord God is my strength;
He will make my feet like deer's feet,
And He will make me walk on my high hills
(3:17-19).

I don't know all that much about olive crops or fig trees, but I know something about suffering. I know something about pain and sorrow. And I know that God has been faithful to me even when I have been unfaithful to Him. Dr. Charles Stanley calls it trusting God in the dark.

"In difficult times, faith becomes a matter of devoted allegiance to the Lord Jesus Christ," he writes. "Do we have confidence in Him regardless of the circumstances?"[1]

I kept a journal throughout this adventure, and this book is compiled from stories I wrote and adapted along the journey. I was forced to examine my spiritual heart and I had to ask myself that question: *Did I have confidence in God regardless of my circumstances?* Looking back, I discovered there was a lot to laugh at and there was a lot to cry over. And there were plenty of opportunities for me to learn life lessons from the Lord.

Like many Southern storytellers, I'm prone to exaggerate to make a point and, as you will discover, that is the case in this book. My story is based on fact, but some episodes were crafted from my imagination.

This is not a story about heart surgery. It's not a story about running a marathon. It's a story about living life. So welcome to my journey. Feel free to grab some iced tea, a plate of barbecue, and get ready to dig in. My name is Todd Starnes. I survived heart surgery. I ran a marathon. I am a follower of Jesus Christ, and this is *my* story.

ENDNOTE
[1]Charles F. Stanley, *The Charles F. Stanley Life Principles Bible* (Nashville: Thomas Nelson, 2005) 1075.

1

You Have a Big Heart!

"Mr. Starnes, you have a big heart."

I was a bit surprised. I hardly knew the attending physician in Sutter Medical Center's emergency room. Nevertheless, I thanked him for his compliment and explained to him that I try to attend church once a week, donate to a variety of charities, and help my fellow man.

"That's not what I meant," he replied. "Your heart is enlarged."

That was the first indication something was wrong. For weeks I had been feeling lethargic. I hadn't had a good night's sleep in ages, and to make matters worse, I had developed a terrible cough. I figured it was because of my hefty frame. It's not easy hauling around three hundred pounds.

"Why is it enlarged?" I asked.

The doctor shrugged his shoulders. "I don't know," he said. "But we're going to need to find out. This is serious. We need to run some tests."

Within a matter of days, I discovered there was a *very* serious problem—my aortic valve was in the final stages of failure. The aortic valve is responsible for letting blood flow exit the heart. The typical aortic valve has three flaps; mine had two. It was a quirk in genetics—one that was not caught when I was born and was left undetected until now. Because my aortic valve was not fully opening, my heart was having to work overtime to force blood through the narrow valve.

The diagnosis was severe. My heart valve was not salvageable. It needed to be replaced, and that meant open-heart surgery. I sort of laughed off the doctor's dire warning. I told him the surgery would need to wait until after the summer. After all, I'd just moved to Sacramento and I was in the middle of a busy political season at the state capitol.

The doctor stared directly into my eyes and told me something that sent a chill down my spine. "Listen to me," he said, "if you do not have this surgery, you will die. It may not be next week or next month, but without this surgery you may not make it through the summer."

The doctor had my undivided attention. "And your weight is going to be an issue," he said. "We may need to do bypass surgery as well. And we also need to talk about the significant risk of a stroke. Todd, you're going to face a very difficult time."

"It's bucking-up time," Dad used to say during those moments that required an extra measure of fortitude. This was going to be one of those times. I'm not sure what else the doctor told me that day. I was still sorting out the part about imminent death.

I walked outside the doctor's office, sat down on a park bench, and pulled out my cell phone. "Dad, it's me. I'm afraid I have some bad news." All of a sudden I abandoned my cavalier spirit and broke down. I can't remember ever crying as much as I cried that afternoon. And even though he was twenty-five hundred miles away, Dad gave me a shoulder to lean on as I poured out my worries.

Dad knew something about the journey I was about to embark on. It's one he had taken a few years before when he had to have open-heart surgery. Dad told me it was going to be a tough journey—but it was a journey I would not have to make by myself. He reminded me that Jesus promised to be there even in the difficult days of our lives. I knew that promise was true, but I wasn't so sure I believed it. I had faced adversity in my life, but nothing that seemed so insurmountable. I couldn't do a single thing to change my fate. No amount of diet, exercise, or scripture memory could change the fact that my future was out of my hands. "Courage," Dad said, "you need to find courage."

The Lord spoke about courage in Joshua 1:6: "Be strong and of good courage."

The Lord spoke those words to Joshua three times in chapter 1. Joshua didn't have a heart condition, but he did have some fairly difficult issues—like wandering around in the wilderness for forty years. It wasn't exactly a walk in the park.

Dr. Charles Stanley argues that Christians need courage to keep our balance, writing, "In any case, we can trust the Holy Spirit to help us in times of adversity and to grow and change so that we can live in keeping with the example set by Jesus Christ."[1]

He calls adversity a boot camp, "rigorous, painful, and challenging."[2] That seemed to define my future. Not only would I be faced with open-heart surgery, but I was going to be forced to make some other decisions—like losing weight and living a healthy life. "If you don't," my doctor said, "you will not live a very long life—even with a new heart valve." He told me I had a choice. I could keep scarfing down Big Macs or I could get off the couch and start living a heart-healthy life.

I can relate to Joshua. In a way, I've been living in a spiritual wilderness for the past forty years. I've always wanted to follow God's call on my life, but there have been many times when I wasn't quite sure if I was. My spiritual walk was more like a roller-coaster ride—there were ups and downs. Erratic is a good way to describe it.

Confucius said a journey of a thousand miles begins with a single step—one single step! Maybe this was my opportunity to step out in true faith and trust God. Maybe this was the moment I could do as God commanded: "Be strong and of good courage." Maybe this was the moment to recommit my life and my body to God's will.

The journey was certain to be rigorous and painful—and definitely challenging. But it was time to step out in faith and believe that God would direct my path. It was time to surrender my will for His.

As Paul teaches us in Philippians 3:8-11,

> Yet indeed I also count all things loss for the excellence of the knowledge of Christ Jesus my Lord, for whom I have suffered the loss of all things, and count them as rubbish, that I may gain Christ and be found in Him, not having my own righteousness, which is from the law, but that which is through faith in Christ, the righteousness which is from God by faith; that I may know Him and the power of His resurrection, and the fellowship of His sufferings, being conformed to His death, if, by any means, I may attain to the resurrection from the dead.

For a moment, I was consumed with a gentle spirit of peacefulness. My greatest fear was death and yet, as a believer, I know that death has been conquered. And so, on that warm spring afternoon, I came face-to-face with my fear and found myself humming a familiar tune.

There's a land that is fairer than day, and by faith
we can see it afar;

For the Father waits over the way, to prepare us a
dwelling place there.
In the sweet by-and-by, we shall meet on that
beautiful shore;
In the sweet by-and-by, we shall meet on that
beautiful shore.

In other words, my fear of death had just lost
its sting.

ENDNOTES

[1]Charles F. Stanley, *The Charles F. Stanley Life Principles Bible* (Nashville: Thomas Nelson, 2005) 242.
[2]*Ibid.*

2

DEAR JESUS, THANK YOU FOR BUTTER!

"I hate butter!"

My declaration was met with stunned silence around the Starnes family table. I was just a little boy, not even seven years old, and my taste buds had not yet adjusted to the taste of cold yellow slabs of butter pasted onto fluffy biscuits.

Mom was flustered. "What do you mean you don't like butter? Of course you like butter. We're from the South. We're supposed to love butter."

Indeed, a Southern boy not liking butter is akin to a kid in the Bronx not liking the Yankees. Uncle Jerry was so shocked he stopped gnawing on his pork chop and declared, "There's something wrong with that boy." Uncle Jerry is from Coldwater, Mississippi, and folks there are prone to say things like that. "I told you that boy was too skinny."

After recovering from the initial shock of the moment, Mom did what any God-fearing mom would do. "We should pray," she said.

"But we've already prayed, honey," said Dad. "Besides, the potatoes are getting cold."

But when Mom said it was time to pray, it was time to pray. The entire family joined hands and bowed our heads. "Dear Jesus," Mom petitioned the Almighty, "thank You for butter. Thank You for giving us the cows that gave us butter. And thank You, Lord, for buttermilk biscuits on which we can place a dollop of butter. Because, Lord, we know that somewhere in the world tonight little children are going to bed without any butter at all. Amen."

Well, good grief! I was just seven years old. I didn't want to disappoint my mom and I sure didn't want to disappoint Jesus. So that day I started eating butter—and never stopped.

I am a son of the South. I was born in Memphis and raised in Mississippi. We lay claim to Ole Miss, William Faulkner, and fried catfish. We are not the most educated state and we are not the wealthiest state, but Mississippi does lay claim to being the nation's fattest state. There are a number of reasons for our well-rounded status. First and foremost, Southerners love to eat more than we like to exercise.

Let's be honest—given the choice of eating cornbread with Paula Deen or sweating to the oldies with Richard Simmons, most of us would ask for a cast-iron skillet in a heartbeat.

And Southern women know how to cook. Some of my dearest memories revolve around family dinners. Mom and my grandmother could lay out a spread! Roast beef, fried chicken, buttermilk biscuits, sweet potato pie, mustard greens—sweet mercy!

I was especially fond of dinner-on-the-grounds. I grew up Southern Baptist—a denomination known for fighting and food. We do both so well. Every month that had a fifth Sunday would result in a fellowship meal called dinner-on-the-grounds. After a morning of preaching, the ladies would convene on the churchyard to assemble what seemed like miles and piles of food. Once the head of the Woman's Missionary Union declared the meal was ready to be served, the preacher would deliver grace and then we were off to the races.

I always tried to scamper to the front of the line to grab some of Mom's deviled eggs and sweet potato casserole. Her selections always went fast. And, for the rest of the day, the congregation tapped their toes to a gospel quartet and devoured so much fried chicken it would've made Colonel Sanders blush.

I'm not quite sure how we managed to do it, but Southerners have figured out a way to deep-fry the entire food pyramid—from fried pork chops to deep-fried green beans.

Those are fond memories, but they are also sad memories. As many times as I heard preachers admonish us about the dangers of hitting the bottle, I never heard a preacher tell us about another sin—gluttony. And judging from the size of some of our church deacons, I have a pretty good idea why preachers steer clear of such sermons.

Obesity is nothing to laugh about. It's killing our nation, it's killing our fellow brothers and sisters in Christ, and it almost killed me. Granted, there are some people who have legitimate medical conditions that account for their girth. But let's be honest, most of us just have a bad case of "food-in-mouth" disease!

My cardiologist had a Come-to-Jesus meeting with me a few days before my surgery. He told me I was lucky. I was going to get a second chance at life. He told me I had a choice. I could keep on stuffing my face and die early—or I could make some heart-healthy changes in my lifestyle and live a long and productive life.

It didn't take me terribly long to figure out what I needed to do. I decided it was time to put down the Big Mac. It was time to say goodbye to the Krispy Kreme doughnut, and it was time to bid a fond farewell to that plate of scattered, smothered, and covered at the Waffle House.

Later I will explain how I lost all the weight, but right now I issue a call to my fellow Christians: Put down the fried chicken leg, step away from the buffet, and wipe the chocolate sauce from your lips. The body of Christ, my friends, is a bit too big!

3

GO WEST, YOUNG MAN!

There are no fat people in California. I'm not sure why, but it could have something to do with their steady diet of tofu and tree bark. And a fairly sizable chunk of the state appears to be the offspring of George Hamilton. I've never seen so many well-tanned Americans.

And then, there was me—a three-hundred-pound white guy with a pale complexion and a Southern accent. I could just imagine the horror at the Sacramento Chamber of Commerce. "Well, there goes the neighborhood." I felt like a catfish at a sushi bar.

I sure hope I made the right decision.

My Ford Taurus was packed tighter than a shirt on Dolly Parton and I was driving about five miles an hour through midtown Sacramento trying to find my new apartment. It was a scene straight out of *The Beverly Hillbillies*. Finally, I waved down a police officer.

"You must not be from around here," he said. "What gave it away?" I asked, "My weight or my pasty white skin?"

"Your license plate," he said. "You're from Tennessee."

The officer went above and beyond the call of duty. He told me to follow him and he would take me to my apartment. "Welcome to California," he said. "We're not all fruits and nuts."

"Why in the world would you want to go to California?" Dad asked. "They're all just a bunch of fruits and nuts."

I wasn't surprised by Dad's reaction. I had lived my entire life in the South. I was born in Memphis, was raised in Mississippi, went to high school in Louisiana, and started my journalism career in Georgia. When I was a kid, I dreamed of owning a weekly newspaper in a small town like Mayberry. That was *my* dream. It wasn't God's.

I had been offered a job in Northern California at one of the top news radio stations in the nation—KFBK. It was where Morton Downey Jr. once worked, and it was where Rush Limbaugh launched what would become his national radio show. If I was going to make any kind of an impact in news radio, I needed to get to Sacramento.

How I got to KFBK is something of a miracle—not as big as the loaves and fishes or even the water into wine (or grape juice), but it was a pretty big miracle in my life.

I started the radio part of my journalism career in 2004 at WTJS in Jackson, Tennessee. I loved that little radio station. The news talker was part of a cluster of three stations owned by Clear Channel. And even though WTJS ran Rush Limbaugh and Sean Hannity, it was dead last in the ratings. WTJS didn't even have any ratings.

The new general manager, Roger Vestal, saw potential in the AM station, so he offered me a job as their news director. Unfortunately, the pay wasn't all that great. Jackson is one of the smallest radio markets in the nation—ranked 293. And even worse, the station had a big fat goose egg of a rating. So I made a deal with Roger. If I could turn around the station's ratings within one book, he would meet my salary request. Roger accepted the deal, and I became the news director and program director at WTJS—a station that shared my initials, Todd James Starnes.

I want to establish an undisputed fact: I had absolutely no idea what I was doing. I was literally walking by faith. I knew how to do the news, but programming a radio station was way above my pay grade (minimal as it was). So, here's the plan I came up with: program the station with stuff I liked—live local news, sports, and weather—and promote the heck out of our all-star lineup of Rush Limbaugh and Sean Hannity.

But it was going to take time to build a solid audience, and I didn't have time. I had one ratings book to change the station's destiny. Otherwise, I would be living at the station—in a broom closet. We had completely overhauled the sound of WTJS. It was young, it was hip, the music was upbeat, the news was fast, and we branded ourselves as "Smart Radio for Smart People." We even added a professional weather forecaster, Dave Hacker, who also happened to be our chief engineer. For the record, Dave's forecasts were more accurate than his television counterparts (and he had nicer hair).

The locals were beginning to take notice, but we still needed something really big to get folks talking about our station. And then, Mel Gibson walked into my life. If the South is the Bible Belt, Jackson is the buckle—with churches and Christian universities everywhere. So we made sure to cover the region's religion news. And the big religion story was the upcoming release of *The Passion of the Christ*. The movie was set to debut in Jackson and it was the talk of the town. That's when I had my epiphany.

"We should scoop up as many tickets as possible and give them away on the air," I told my boss.

"It's a great idea, but we don't have any cash," was his reply.

There was absolutely no money for the tiny AM station, especially since Clear Channel owned two 100,000-watt FM stations. There were financial priorities at stake.

That's when I did something that made absolutely no sense whatsoever. I decided that if Clear Channel couldn't buy tickets for a giveaway, I would buy the tickets. But I took it one step further—I decided to buy every opening-night ticket. I figured if we were going to make an impact in the city, we would need to do something bold. To finance my idea, I cashed in my 401(k) and rented an entire movie theatre. And for the two weeks leading up to the film, I gave away every single ticket on air.

We were building our core audience one ticket at a time, and by opening night, the buzz was beginning to spread. *The Passion of the Christ* was a powerful film and it made a powerful impact on WTJS.

I had taken an incredible gamble, really stepping out in faith and doing something that was pretty foolish. Yet, I felt a peace about what I was doing and I believed I was doing the right thing.

A few weeks later, my expectations were confirmed. WTJS, the tiny AM radio station, was no longer a bottom-dweller. We had gone from a zero share to a four share in one ratings book! It was a miracle! The station was not only attracting listeners, but it was also attracting advertisers, and thanks to an incredible team of radio experts, WTJS had become a major player in the market.

Our success also helped boost my very young radio career, and I began sending out air-checks to some radio stations in larger markets. Two of those air-checks were sent to markets on the

West Coast. One was in Sacramento and the other was in one of the Rocky Mountain states. I received a telephone call from them first.

The news director said she liked my work, but she was especially disturbed by my voice. "You really have an accent," she said. "It's bad. I'm afraid people in our city wouldn't be able to take you seriously."

I was devastated—glad she was being honest, but still devastated. "What do you recommend I do?"

"You need to hire a vocal coach and get rid of your Southern accent," she said. "Otherwise, you will never be able to work west of Dallas."

I hung up the phone and was fairly dejected. I didn't think my accent was all that bad, but maybe it was. Maybe I was just meant to be at WTJS for the rest of my career. I was okay with that. It was a great station and the people were absolute angels.

A few weeks had gone by when I received another telephone call. This one was from KFBK in Sacramento. It was one of the nation's biggest news talkers—50,000 watts of power. At night, you can hear their signal from Alaska to New Mexico.

"This is Alan Eisenson," said the voice on the other end of the line. "We heard your stuff."

I was prepared to hear him explain why I was being turned down, but instead he said, "We like it. It's pretty good. How would you like a job in Sacramento?"

I dropped the phone.

"Hello? Hello?"

"Uh, sorry about that. I dropped the phone. You heard my stuff? You listened to my stuff?"

"Yes. It's what we're looking for," he said. "So, do you want to come out West?"

And in a matter of about a year, I went from Market 293 to Market 27.

The hard part was telling my folks. They lived in Georgia, and while my visits home were few and far between, I loved talking to them on the phone and always saw them at Christmas.

"Are you sure you want to do this?" Dad asked. "It's a really different world out there."

I told him I was pretty sure that God was leading me to the West Coast. I wasn't sure why, but I felt I needed to go. Eventually, Dad came around and told me he was very proud. "Just promise me you'll stay away from San Francisco," he said. "Some of those folks just aren't right."

I mapped out a journey that would take me along I-40 through Oklahoma, Texas, Arizona, New Mexico, Nevada, and Southern California. From there, I would take I-5 out of Los Angeles all the way to Sacramento. But first, I needed to stop in Memphis to visit my grandmother.

We call her Mema. Her given name is Lucile. My great-grandfather was hoping for a son, so he nicknamed her Billie. She was the original

43

Steel Magnolia. There's no doubt that she relishes her role as the quiet matriarch of our sprawling family. When she speaks—everyone listens. She distinguished herself at home and church. She was an accomplished seamstress and baker. She grew award-winning roses and played golf at the country club. She's traveled around the world. And she means the world to me.

I am particularly close to my grandmother. She's followed my career from the beginning, and she's always held on to a belief that God is ultimately in control. Her faith has been unwavering. And it was her faith in me that would propel me through the days that were to come.

One of my fondest memories involves a trip my grandmother took to south Florida with some of her girlfriends. All of them were in their early to mid-eighties. These golden girls saw advertisements for Senior Week in Daytona Beach. They thought it would be fun to take a road trip from their retirement home in Memphis.

They had driven as far as Batesville, Mississippi, when they were pulled over for doing forty in a seventy-mile-an-hour zone.

"What seems to be the problem, officer?"

"Well, you were going a bit too slow, ladies. Where are you heading?"

"Daytona Beach," said one of my grandmother's girlfriends.

"At this time of year? Are you sure you want to do that? It's spring break. That place is going to be packed."

"Oh, we know, officer! It's Senior Week. And Billie is hoping to meet up with Andy Griffith. He's Matlock, you know."

It didn't take the officer long to deduce an undeniable fact: these ladies had no idea what they were heading into. He wrote them a warning ticket and told them to put the pedal to the metal.

My grandmother has a thing for Matlock. She watches that show like clockwork and has entire episodes committed to memory. The running joke on their trip was whether she could find Matlock partying somewhere on the beach.

I'm relieved to report that all four of the golden girls survived spring break in Daytona. They assured me there was no hanky-panky, and although they were invited to at least one kegger, they declined the invitation. It was past their bedtime. They were less than forthcoming about an alleged incident involving their balcony and a swimsuit competition. I've been advised by the ladies to drop the subject.

Some of us weren't all that keen on the idea of Mema driving to Daytona, and I was bold enough to express my objections. She quietly listened and then told me something that I've never forgotten.

"You only live once and you need to embrace life," she said. "Just because you're old doesn't mean you're dead."

In other words, live a life worth living. Take chances. Step out in faith and follow God's call—whether it's to spring break in Daytona or to Northern California. I gave my grandmother a big hug, waved goodbye, got in my car, and headed due west.

When in Rome, do as the Romans, and when in Los Angeles, do as the—well, whatever they call themselves. I decided it was time for me to try some of the local cuisine. I stopped at this snazzy Japanese restaurant off Sunset Boulevard.

The waitress brought out a tray of raw fish, cold rice, and a dipping sauce that cleared out my sinus cavities.

"Is there anything else you desire?"

"Yes," I replied. "I'd like some vegetable oil and a deep fryer. Somebody forgot to cook this fish."

"It's supposed to be like that, sir. It's sushi."

There's something just not right about eating raw fish. That's why God gave us grease. They could've at least tossed in a few hush puppies.

This California living may take some getting used to, I decided.

4

PIG OR PLASTIC?

You can call me the quarter-million-dollar man. I may not have bionic body parts like Steve Austin, but I was about to get a spiffy graphite aortic valve. My insurance company said the valve is worth about $250,000 (wash and wax not included).

"So we need to talk about this new heart valve," my heart surgeon said. "We've got a couple of directions we can go, and I'm going to let you decide which kind of valve you want."

My doctor handed me a few shiny pamphlets extolling the wonderful world of artificial body parts. For a moment, I thought I was in a car dealership looking to accessorize my ride.

Basically, there are two kinds of heart valves—artificial and biological. The artificial valves are typically made from a graphite plastic material that has a life span of about two hundred years.

The biological valves are normally harvested from pigs.

It took me about five seconds to decide which kind I wanted. "Oh, I'm all about the pig valve," I told him. The sheer entertainment value alone would be worth the surgery. And I thought my passion for barbecue would be complete—the pig and I would be one.

"Yeah, well you might want to reconsider," my surgeon told me. "Pig valves only last about fourteen years. I'm not too sure that you want to have open-heart surgery every decade."

Suddenly, the graphite valve didn't seem so bad after all. Besides, the doctor said that my new heart valve would outlast me. There would be some risks, though. The mechanical heart valve would require a significant change in my lifestyle. I would have to take blood thinners for the rest of my life because the mechanical valve puts me at risk for deadly clots. That means a pretty strict diet, weekly blood tests, and absolutely no body-contact sports. A common nosebleed could result in a visit to the emergency room, and "living dangerously" meant shaving with a razor. I was going to have to be very careful, my doctor said.

We spent a good part of the afternoon going over the intricate details of the surgery, my recovery, and the side effects of the medicines that would keep me running on all my cylinders. It was a physically and mentally exhausting day.

I drove back to my apartment in midtown Sacramento, tossed the mail on the coffee table, grabbed the remote, and promptly fell asleep during a rerun of *The Dukes of Hazzard*. The next thing I knew, I was being hoisted onto a rack inside Cooter's Garage.

"Breaker one, breaker one. Okay, boys, plop that big'un up here on the rack. I wanna get a good look at his undercarriage."

I was slightly confused (to say the least). "What's going on here?"

"Hey there, big'un, and welcome to Cooter's Garage. Heard you were in need of a valve job. Bo and Luke found you broke down on the side of the road and I towed you in. Now, don't you worry. Ol' Cooter will have you up and running in no time."

I watched as Cooter poked and prodded. He nodded his head a few times, took off his hat, and then let out a big shout. "Good Lord, boy!"

"What? What did you find, Cooter?"

"Well, I popped your hood and found gravy on the dipstick."

"How do you suppose we can fix it?"

"Well, I've got an idea. Nurse Daisy? Get me a couple of buttermilk biscuits. We need to mop up this gravy spill."

Nurse Daisy came in wearing her trademark cutoff jeans and shapely T-shirt. "Comin' right up, Cooter."

"On second thought, forget the biscuits, Daisy. We've got ourselves a big problem here. This boy's plumbing is all messed up. You'd better toss me a jigsaw and give that boy a swig of Uncle Jesse's moonshine. I'm gonna have to open him up like a Thanksgiving Day turkey."

"Are you crazy?" I shouted. "This is a gas station, not a hospital."

Cooter replied, "Boy, I may be crazy, but I'm not dumb. Now hush up. Oh boy!"

"What's wrong now?"

"Daisy, stand back. We've got ourselves a gusher. Grab me one of them pig valves and a jar of barbecue sauce. And make it quick. This is going to be one heck of a lube job."

I heard Waylon Jennings intone, "Now friends, that just ain't right."

Just before Cooter was about to carve me up, we went to a commercial break and I woke up shouting, "Daisy, save me!" Alas, Daisy wasn't there—and fortunately neither was Cooter. It was all just a bad dream.

Sweet mercy, I thought. *If I make it through this alive, I'm going to need therapy.*

5

THERE'S A DRAFT IN
THIS GOWN!

I had to write my will. I believe it's pretty safe to say that any day you have to write your will is a bad day. At this point, I'm not sure what's more depressing—writing the will or discovering I'm actually worth more dead than alive.

The days leading up to my surgery would be anything but relaxing. I had to fill out all sorts of paperwork ranging from long-term disability forms to life insurance policies. I also had to complete a living will. I wanted to leave my family very clear instructions on what to do if the surgery was less than successful. These were difficult decisions to make—especially for someone in his thirties.

I'm a news reporter. I'm used to covering life-and-death matters every day. It's part of the job. But when my mortality is the story—well, that's a totally different matter. The living will was not a big issue for me. I am pro-life. That means every life is precious—inside and outside the womb.

I scratched and scribbled a number of drafts, but it was just way too difficult. So I decided to do what I normally do when I don't want to do something—I went shopping.

I had a valid reason for going shopping. I needed to purchase a new pair of pajamas. I was going to be in the hospital for quite some time and I was determined not to wear one of those drafty gowns. The last thing I wanted to do was inadvertently moon the entire cardiac wing. That would have just been unfortunate.

I spent a good half hour wandering in and out of shops at our mall. I finally ended up at one of those high-end retailers—the kind with real piano players in the lobby. A salesclerk directed me to their men's pajama department. The choices were slim.

"Do you have anything in guy colors?"

"We have a lovely red silk two-piece."

"What else do you have?"

"The only other thing in your size would be these SpongeBob pajamas."

That would be SpongeBob SquarePants, the cartoon character. I wondered if maybe I should just get a fluffy bathrobe instead.

I should've been amused, but my mind was still grappling over the will. I'm not quite sure why it was so hard for me to finish it. It wasn't necessarily deciding who gets what (Uncle Jerry gets first dibs on the SpongeBob pajamas). I sat down in my living room and began compiling a list of all my stuff—and there was a bunch of stuff. The longer my list grew, the more I became convinced that I had not been a very good steward of God's provisions for my life.

And that's pretty much what a will is—an official accounting of the stuff you've accumulated over the years. And most of the stuff I had collected was pretty much worthless (except for my copy of the exclusive director's cut of *The Godfather I, II,* and *III*).

Scanning my list, I wondered if I'd been taking stock in all the wrong things. I've made my fair share of financial investments. Some were good, like a new washing machine. Some were not so good, like the Ab Rocker. The guy on television promised me I would have hard, sleek abs with just five minutes a day. I'm still waiting for my cash back on that one.

But, I asked myself, what had I been doing about the investments that really matter? What kind of investments had I made in the work of God's kingdom?

Over the years, I've been pretty involved in the work of the church. I've taught Sunday school, sang in the choir, and gone on more mission trips than I can remember. But I found myself wondering if I could have done more.

That's the point of the will. If things turned unpleasant on May 17, the will would serve as a testament to the kind of person I was. I wondered if people would look at my list and see a person who spent more money on his movie collection than on his local church. Would they see a person who invested his time in the work of the kingdom of God?

My thoughts were interrupted by the sales-clerk.

"Sir, have you made a selection?"

"Well, I'm wondering about these SpongeBob pajamas. What do you think?"

"Frankly, sir, I wouldn't be caught dead in them."

"That's what I'm afraid of."

6

THE LAST SUPPER

"We must have a party!"

My friend Jeannine was quite the party planner. She could turn any occasion into a festive event at the drop of a hat. "It's not every day you have heart surgery, so we should celebrate."

And that's how I ended up at Sacramento's Tower Café on the evening before my operation. It was an event Jeannine called "The Last Supper."

I met Tom and Jeannine Sommers at the First Baptist Church of Fair Oaks. One Sunday morning the pastor asked me to share a word about Henry Blackaby's book *Experiencing God*. Afterward, I was approached by a very excited couple who just had to meet me. It was Tom and Jeannine. They had been visiting the church and, by coincidence, had also read *Experiencing God*.

Before I could get a word in edgewise, Jeannine had already made plans for me to join them at their home for lunch and dinner. They lived in a well-heeled part of Sacramento in the city's historic Land Park, and Jeannine proved to be the quintessential hostess. It was as if the Lord took the genetic fabric of Paula Deen, Martha Stewart, and Beth Moore and created Jeannine.

I'll never forget our first meal—turkey tacos with homemade taco shells and guacamole. By the time dessert rolled around, the Sommerses had adopted me as one of their own.

"I'm your West Coast mom," she boldly proclaimed. Over the months we enjoyed frequent outdoor dinners at the Tower Café, where we talked about politics, the Bible, and all sorts of lighthearted topics. But one day I learned something very interesting about Jeannine. She spoke the truth—wrapped in a healthy dose of love.

"Todd," she told me one day, "you are obese."

I wasn't quite sure how to respond. "Thank you" seemed a bit out of order, and "Yeah, well you're old" would have definitely been out of line. I was taken aback by her brutal honesty, but a part of me appreciated that she cared enough about me to rattle my world.

Tom and Jeannine were very active. They went skiing in Tahoe and jogged through Land Park. Physical fitness was a big part of their lives. Jeannine told me I needed to consider my health.

"You never know what could happen," she said. "You need to turn this over to God."

I smiled and told her I would consider it. I supposed I could stand to lose a few pounds.

It was hard to believe we had that conversation just a few weeks before, and now we were celebrating my "last supper." I smiled as I remembered Jeannine's prophetic utterances. I was glad to be with friends. I needed to be around friends, and I was especially glad to see Michael at our table.

I've known Michael Winn for almost ten years. He showed up one day, tried out for a church play that I was directing, and the rest is history. He's one of those brooding artist-musician types. It took about three months for him to start talking, but once he did, I discovered he was probably one of the deepest and most intellectual friends I had. Our personalities are polar opposites, but for some reason, we struck up a friendship that has lasted through good times and bad.

So it was not a surprise when he flew out from Nashville to hang out with me the week before the surgery. We hiked across the Golden Gate Bridge, caught some comedy shows in San Francisco, and faithfully observed a ritual of our friendship watching *The Godfather* and eating Italian food. He has been a friend who has always been there, and that night he was in Sacramento and I was glad.

"Aren't you excited, Todd?" Jeannine asked. "This is the start of a new life for you. The Lord is giving you a second chance. I bet you can't wait to start losing all that weight. You are going to be a new skinny man."

I wished I shared Jeannine's enthusiasm, but I could not shake a feeling of pending doom. I would've given anything to drown my sorrows in a package of Nutter Butters. But Jeannine was right. I needed to start losing weight. So, why not start now?

I may as well take the plunge and start my new fat-free life. The waitress came and took our orders. And, for the first time in my life, I did the unthinkable. I ordered a salad and a glass of unsweetened iced tea.

"That's pretty extreme," said Michael.

Jeannine dabbed the tears from her eyes.

"Oh, this is wonderful news," she said. "We should pray."

We all joined hands as Tom delivered thanks over our meal. I figured I should offer a silent petition to the Almighty.

Lord, please don't let this be my last supper.

I tossed and turned all night. My doctor told me I needed to get a good night's rest, but it was impossible. I had way too much on my mind. I lay in bed and stared at the clock for hours. Still, I was startled when my alarm sounded at five o'clock the next morning.

After two weeks of poking and prodding, worry and dread, it was time. The plan was for

Pastor Wayne and Nancy to pick me up and drive me to Sutter Memorial Hospital. I had to be in pre-op by six.

Michael had been sleeping on my couch all week. He was already up and about as I packed a suitcase and took one final look around my apartment. Just before we walked out the door, Michael came over and put his hand on my shoulder.

"Nervous?"

"Yeah."

"It's going to be okay, you know."

"I know."

Well, that wasn't exactly true. I had no idea if it was going to be okay, and neither did Michael. But that's what you're supposed to say whenever somebody is about to go under the knife.

What Michael really meant to say was, "I sure hope you aren't dead tomorrow."

Michael tried to offer a few words of encouragement. "You know, you're going to get a pretty good scar out of all this."

It reminded me of the line from an old football movie—"Chicks dig scars."

"Wanna pray?"

"Nervous?"

"Yeah."

For a few brief moments, two brothers in Christ talked to the Lord. And for the first time in a while, I felt a sense of deep and abiding peace. We walked out of my apartment and I turned to Michael and said, "Thank you for being here."

"Wouldn't have missed it," he said. "Besides, how cool is it to have your heart surgery in Northern California? We're just an hour from Tahoe!"

7

THE BARBER OF SEVILLE

"I am the Barber of Seville!"

The physician's assistant really knew how to make an entrance. He was wearing green surgical scrubs and a rather unorthodox cap made from some sort of fabric with a tropical-bird theme.

The room was filled with folks from the church—Pastor Wayne and Nancy, Tom and Jeannine, and Michael. They were getting a front-row view of the indecencies inflicted on heart patients. "I think this is going to be pretty good," said Pastor Wayne.

The man in green scrubs snapped to attention at my bedside and repeated his declaration. "I am the Barber of Seville and I am here to give you a shave."

I smiled, but declined his offer. I told him I had shaved before coming to the hospital. He let out a loud laugh and shook his head.

"You don't understand. I'm here to shave everything," he said.

"What do you mean by 'everything'?"

"*Everything.*"

That's when Michael made the decision I wish I could've made. "Okay, that's it for me. See you guys downstairs in the cafeteria."

I swallowed hard and tried to consider my options, which were limited. By that time a nurse had hooked up a garden hose to my arm.

"It's for the drugs," she said. "You won't feel a thing." Apparently no one had ever tried shoving a garden hose up her arm. The pain was so intense my back arched upward.

Sweet mercy! This is going to make heart surgery seem like a piece of cake.

Bolting for the front door was no longer an option. I was resigned to the fact that a strange guy in a Toucan Sam hat was about to shave my chest and armpits. It wasn't all that bad, and for a second I chided myself for getting worked up into such a lather. He stopped just short of my belly button.

"Well, that wasn't so bad," I said. "Sorry I made such a big deal about it."

"We aren't finished," he replied.

"What do you mean 'We aren't finished'?"

"I have to shave down there," he said.

"Down where?"

"Where the sun doesn't shine."

The church folks were thoroughly entertained. "How about that," said Nancy. "You're getting a full-body shave!"

Jeannine couldn't control herself. "Does that include a bikini wax?"

"I'm not sure that's covered on his insurance plan," Nancy replied.

I strongly protested, telling the Barber of Seville that doing so would violate one of the basic tenets of my faith.

Pastor Wayne interjected: "No, no, I don't think so. There's nothing in the church bylaws prohibiting a full-body shave."

"Out," I demanded. "You must leave right now!"

The ladies were enjoying every minute. "We're just having some fun," said Nancy as the barber herded them into a waiting room.

Could I please get someone with the spiritual gift of mercy at my bedside?

I want to stop for just a moment and let you in on a tiny secret: I am extremely ticklish. If someone even pretends to tickle me, I will break out in uncontrollable laughter and convulsions. I am especially ticklish on my legs. And, as the Barber of Seville was about to discover, that was going to be problematic.

I nearly jerked out of the bed when he tried to shave my kneecap, and my left toe almost became lodged in his nose. The Barber of Seville was growing a bit frustrated. The closer he got, the more I started wiggling and laughing. He picked up a phone and called for a nurse. There was only one way he was going to be able to finish his job—drugs.

The nurse came into my room and gave me a mild sedative.

"Those drugs should be doing their job right about now," she said. "Are you feeling a bit more relaxed?"

I wasn't quite sure. I felt like I was cartwheeling across the room with Sgt. Pepper's Lonely Hearts Club Band. Strange colors swirled around and around and around.

And why is everyone talking in slow motion?

Once I was loaded up on an adequate dosage of "happy juice," the Barber of Seville finished his work. Within a few minutes he proclaimed, "Smoother than a newborn baby!"

By then, I was slowly coming back down to Earth and my drug-induced fog was beginning to clear. The nurse checked my vitals. "Mr. Starnes, are you still with us? Are you okay?"

I wasn't so sure. I felt like a modern-day equivalent of Samson. It's a good thing there weren't any donkey jawbones lying around. I had been stripped of my hair and my dignity. And, for some strange reason, I had a bad case of the munchies.

8

DEAR GOD, PLEASE DON'T LET ME DIE!

Pray without ceasing. That was the admonition the apostle Paul delivered in 1 Thessalonians 5:17. My great-grandfather was a practitioner of that kind of prayer. He once prayed so long over Sunday dinner that the mashed potatoes turned cold.

I'll be the first to admit I don't have a very good prayer life. My petitions to God are random and selfish—usually centering around some sort of pending calamity that I caused in the first place. I don't mean for it to be that way, but sadly, it is. I have a friend who attends an Episcopal church—one that still believes the Bible. He suggested I write a prayer. I wasn't too sold on that idea. I've always felt written prayers to be sort of—well, *canned.*

But who was I to buck several hundred years of tradition? I suppose that each denomination does something better than the next. Church of God folks really know how to worship, Baptists really know how to eat, and Episcopalians—well—they really know how to pray. They even have an entire book of prayers. While I was anything but a "high-church" person, I figured a "low-church" Southern Baptist couldn't do any worse. So I decided to try my hand at writing a prayer.

Besides, I didn't want to go under the knife after uttering a silly prayer like, "God, don't let me die." *That's a bit selfish*, I thought, *a prayer for a simpleton*. No, this was a major event in my life, and it deserved a well-written, well-versed prayer. So I powered up my laptop and invoked my inner Episcopalian:

> Almighty and most holy Father, on this decidedly solemn occasion, I beseech Thee for Thy guidance. You, O God, the Great Healer and Physician, guide the hands of Thy servants as they cutteth upon my anatomy. Give the surgeon precision as he carves Thou humble servant like a Thanksgiving Day turkey. And shouldst Thou see fit, awaken me once the pain subsides. And may I be blessed with a bountiful multitude of legally prescribed narcotics and, if it's not too much trouble, a good-looking nurse in the spirit of Proverbs 31. In the name of the Father, the Son, and the Holy Spirit, amen.

Pretty good stuff, huh?

I printed out a copy and put it in my wallet for safekeeping. The plan was to pull it out and recite it verbatim just before they knocked me out. I figured that should do the trick.

But there was still something that bugged me. I wasn't so sure I deserved to have my prayer answered—or at least answered in the way I wanted. Hundreds, if not thousands, of people across the world are dying every day. People are starving in Third World nations. Lots of folks are a lot worse off than me. So why would God want to be bothered by a guy with a washed-up heart valve?

I thought about that quite a bit in the moments leading up to my surgery. I thought about it as my pastor and church friends gathered around my gurney and joined hands. I thought about it until a nurse came to my side and gently said, "It's time, Mr. Starnes."

And so it was. After two anxiety-filled weeks, I was about to face the biggest challenge of my life. There was no turning back. As my friends held my hands and said their goodbyes, I felt the drugs beginning to flow through my veins. Instinct took over, and my body jerked one way and then another as my eyelids began to flitter. Suddenly, panic set in.

Oh my gosh! The prayer! I forgot the prayer! What was I going to do?

My protestations turned to unintelligible mutters as twilight began to fill the bright-white room. And just before my eyes closed for that final time,

I opened my mouth and whispered, "God, please don't let me die."

And then, I fell asleep.

9

CLOSED FOR REPAIRS

"It's okay, Todd. You're going to sleep. You're going to sleep."

Where's the white light? Isn't there supposed to be a white light?

I was obsessing over the white light—or lack of it. I remember being on a frigid stainless-steel operating table. I remember the drugs coursing through that garden hose hooked up to my arm, and then, I was out. There was nothing but darkness—no bright lights, no angelic voices, and no sign of Elvis.

What the heck is going on?

I thought I would wake up in some sterile white room with Keanu Reeves staring at me, telling me I was in the Matrix. But Keanu wasn't there. I don't even recall floating over my body. The only thing I remember is something the nurse told me just before I went under. "Enjoy the drugs, Todd. They're the best friend you have today."

Within seconds, I was in a deep sleep as a half-dozen surgeons and nurses hooked my body up to all sorts of machines. My eyelids were taped shut. It would take about six hours for them to cut open my chest, remove my defective aortic valve, and install the mechanical valve. It was a risky but necessary surgery. It was risky because of my extreme weight. My doctor was worried that I could have a stroke. It was a risk I had to take. My heartbeat began to slow as my body temperature was medically lowered.

And then, my heart stopped beating.

For the remainder of the surgery, I would be hooked up to a heart-bypass machine. It would take care of keeping me alive as the team worked on my ticker. For the first time in my life, my future was out of my hands. No matter how hard I tried, there was absolutely nothing I could do. I was totally and completely in God's hands.

So how does that organ-donor card work? If they see something they like in there, can they just take it? I really should've gotten some clarification before I went under. Hope I still have my parts when I wake up.

"I'm really sorry, Brother Todd."

The apology came out of left field. I was in the

foyer of our church when a guy came over, put his hand on my shoulder, and apologized.

"We prayed that God would deliver you from this surgery," he said. "We prayed for a miracle—that you would be healed. I guess it just wasn't meant to be."

I thanked him for his concern and encouraged him to keep praying. Later that afternoon, I thought about what he had said. Maybe God had answered his prayer. Maybe the surgery was God's way of healing my body.

Maybe the miracle is that God had gifted the surgical team with the wisdom and tools they needed to fix my heart. Or, could the miracle be the heart-bypass machine that was created to keep me alive?

I believe God is still in the business of miracles. He may not be turning water into wine (or grape juice), but I believe He is still at work. And, I believe God answered the prayers of many people by preparing me and my surgical team for my operation.

The apostle Paul wrote in Philippians 4:19: "And my God shall supply all your need according to His riches in glory by Christ Jesus."

On May 17, the Great Healer and Physician supplied me with a heart-lung machine and a surgical team equipped to repair my aortic valve.

Wait, wait. I think I see something. I see dead people. (Sigh) Trying to hover, but can't get off this table. Is

that music? Oh, no. Is that . . .? No! It can't be. Please, no ABBA!

"So, what kind of music do you want us to play?"

Well, that was an odd question. I was meeting with my surgeon a few days before the operation. He said they like to play music in the operating room. It helps soothe the patient and the medical team.

I asked if he had any suggestions for "music to open your chest to." He suggested Enya. I suggested Lynyrd Skynrd's "Freebird." We compromised and settled for Bach. I have a fairly diverse musical background, so I told the doctor I would be happy with just about anything except ABBA.

I had unpleasant visions of a disco ball dropping from the ceiling as the surgical team changed into spandex outfits and began belting out the lyrics to "Dancing Queen" while somebody cut open my chest with a chain saw.

Fortunately, I'd be able to keep the musical beat with my new heart valve. We had settled on a St. Jude Heart Valve. The valve is sturdy and reliable—unlike pig valves, which have to be replaced every fourteen years. I wasn't all that bothered by the kind of valve they installed. I just told the doctor to give me one that would hold up through the honeymoon. That's one night you sure don't want to blow a valve—if you know what I mean.

Four hours. It's been four hours. What in the world is taking so long? Do these guys get time and a half? Oh, great. I think I have to go to the bathroom.

I was hooked up to at least a half-dozen tubes. There was one for breathing, one for sucking stuff out, one for the drugs, one for going to the bathroom, and a few others protruding from places I didn't even know I had. I was the ultimate couch potato. For the time being, I was being kept alive by machines. My body was closed for repairs.

It was hard to believe that my life had come to a grinding halt because of a tiny valve. As Scripture tells us, if all the parts of the body do not work together—the body doesn't work.

> For in fact the body is not one member but many. If the foot should say, "Because I am not a hand, I am not of the body," is it therefore not of the body? And if the ear should say, "Because I am not an eye, I am not of the body," is it therefore not of the body? If the whole body were an eye, where would be the hearing? If the whole were hearing, where would be the smelling? But now God has set the members, each one of them, in the body just as He pleased. And if they were all one member, where would the body be? (1 Cor. 12:14-19).

Paul was referring to the Christian community in these verses, but his example resonated with me in a very physical way.

My nose itches. Must scratch nose. Must wiggle nose. Don't sneeze. Whatever you do, don't sneeze.

My final flashback takes me to my surgeon's office. He was preparing me for life after the surgery. The recovery would take a long time and it would be very painful. That's not because of the heart valve. It's because of what they had to do to get to the heart valve.

He said they had no choice but to go in through my chest—splitting my sternum right down the middle. I felt woozy.

"We're going to pop you open like a Thanksgiving Day turkey."

I decided if he said something about my stuffing, I would hit him.

He said the toughest part of recovering would be from the chest injury. It would be an arduous process.

"I sure hope you don't have allergies," he said. "Sneezing will be a—well, it will be unpleasant."

The doctor said I would get a heart-shaped pillow that I should press against my chest in the event I had to sneeze. He said it would help soften the blow.

I relayed the information to Dad, who had been through several heart surgeries.

"Tell them to stuff that pillow where the sun doesn't shine," he said. Dad was invoking his inner John the Baptist. "That pillow won't do a thing. Go out and buy a *Strong's Concordance*. Be sure it's a hardback edition. Whenever you need to sneeze, grab the concordance and place it against your chest. It'll help—somewhat."

Dad sneezed two days after his heart surgery. He blew out two staples.

Hey, I think we're in the homestretch. I'm kinda hungry. You guys have room service here? Could somebody stuff a chili dog down my feeding tube?

The surgery was wrapping up. The only thing left to do was suture my incisions. The team used surgical staples to close my chest. I was still heavily medicated and machines were keeping me on this side of eternity. It would be a few more hours before I would be strong enough to breathe on my own. For the moment, I was being sustained through incredibly wonderful medical care and the prayers of hundreds of people across the country. And, even though I was in a deep slumber, I believe I may have managed to utter a brief prayer, too.

Dear Jesus, thank You for legal narcotics.

10

I Need a Woman and Other Tales From the ICCU

My greatest fear is not being in control—those moments when you can't do a blessed thing about the events transpiring around you. And that is exactly where I found myself after eight hours of surgery.

My grandfather survived heart surgery, but he never came off the ventilator. My dad survived heart surgery and had great difficulty coming off the ventilator. My greatest fear was not the heart surgery—it was the ventilator. I had convinced myself I was doomed.

My surgeon tried to be reassuring. "You don't have a thing to worry about," he said. "You'll be sound asleep, and by the time you wake up you will be breathing on your own. You won't even know there was anything shoved down your throat."

So you can imagine my surprise and horror when I woke up in the Intensive Cardiac Care

Unit and I was still hooked up to the ventilator. Even in my heavily drug-induced state, it took me about ten seconds to figure out there was a problem.

Holy cow, I'm still on the ventilator. This can't be good. Oh, no. Something must have happened! The doctor said everything was going to be fine—that I would wake up without the ventilator. And—wait a second—maybe I'm dreaming. Yes, that's it. I'm dreaming. Oh, thank goodness. Ha! Whew! Had myself scared silly for a minute.

And then I heard the voice of a nurse. "Oh, look who decided to wake up. Hi, Todd! You're doing just fine."

So I'm not asleep? This isn't a dream! I'm doomed.

Even though I was semiconscious, I was trying to determine what happened and why I was still on the ventilator.

I must have had a stroke. That's it! I stroked out! Wait a second—if I had a stroke I wouldn't have any reasoning skills, and right now I'm able to reasonably determine whether or not I had a stroke, so I must not have had a stroke. Pen! I need a pen!

I began waving my hand to demonstrate my need for a writing instrument. Michael immediately picked up on my rudimentary sign language skills.

"I think he needs something to write with," he said.

The nurse held a notepad while I composed a memorandum to my caregivers.

To whom it may concern,

If it would not be too much trouble, could someone please remove the tube that is protruding down my throat? It's causing my gag reflex to activate and is most uncomfortable. And I would be most appreciative if you could provide me with a bottle of water.

Yours very truly,
Todd Starnes

It sounded great, but it came out like a second grader's scribble. The nurses never could decipher my note. Neither could my colleagues at KFBK. They were all over the ICU—recording every single beep, gurgle, and movement I made. And they especially wanted to be there to record the very first words I uttered after surviving the surgery. I had been doing some soul-searching a few days before my operation. What could I say to inspire and encourage our listeners?

First words are important. They make an impression. Take Genesis 1:1 for example: "In the beginning God created the heavens and the earth." Or, how about Neal Armstrong? "One small step for man, one giant leap for mankind."

Of course, my first words carried much less significance—but they were my first words, and I sure didn't want to screw it up by saying something I might regret. I *was* heavily medicated. What if I told the surgeon where he could stick his thermometer? That would be most unfortunate and surely land me on the church prayer list.

When the moment finally came to remove me from the ventilator, a hush fell over the Intensive Cardiac Care Unit. A small crowd gathered around my bedside—friends, doctors, nurses, and the reporters waiting to hear my first utterance after such a life-changing operation. As I took my first deep breath, they all leaned closer to my bed, holding each other's hands, waiting to be inspired.

The nurse asked, "Is there anything you need?"

"Yes," I softly replied. "I need a woman."

11

THE FIRST STEP

"Todd Starnes—you've just survived open-heart surgery. What are you going to do?"

"I'm going to Disney World!" Actually, I wanted to sleep. As it turned out, I wouldn't get to do either.

A stranger appeared at the door. Even in my drug-induced state, his appearance was striking. A tall, slender man with bronze skin, his thick head of jet-black hair was speckled with shades of white. He looked like George Hamilton. "Mr. Starnes, my name is Alphonso. I am your physical therapist, and today you are going to walk."

My voice was still scratchy, but I politely informed him that he must be in the wrong room. I just had heart surgery twenty-four hours ago, I explained.

"Twenty-six hours," he replied in a rich baritone voice, accented with his Latin heritage. "And, today, we walk—together!"

I told him he was nuts. Alphonso brushed aside my insult, and from the look in his eyes I could tell my lack of enthusiasm would not deter his mission. "We need to get you out of that bed so you don't get sicker," he said.

I wasn't sure if I was angry or terrified or both. I wasn't ready to do anything but sleep and enjoy the legal drugs flowing through my veins. I'd just survived open-heart surgery for goodness' sake. And now they wanted me to get up and walk?

Alphonso came to my bedside and gently moved my legs over the edge. The plan was for Alphonso to stand about a foot directly in front of me, and I would stand up and take two small steps. Honestly, it could've been a mile. Either way, it seemed nearly impossible. For some reason, the very idea of getting out of that bed was traumatic, and Alphonso could see fear in my eyes.

"It's okay," he said. "I won't let anything happen to you."

"What if I fall?"

"Then I will catch you."

"What if I can't do it?"

"Then we will try again tomorrow."

"What if . . . ?"

"It will be okay."

The journey of a thousand miles starts with one single step—and this was it. Alphonso helped me out of the bed and, with great trepidation, I steadied my feet on the cold tile floor. Alphonso slowly backed away from me and ordered me to take a step. It seemed like hours, but I moved my left leg first and then my right. I took one step that day and then promptly collapsed into Alphonso's arms. He was ecstatic. "Absolutely wonderful," he said. "That's quite an accomplishment." Yeah, right.

I plopped back into the bed, and as he pulled a blanket over my legs, he said something that seemed outrageous. "You know, Mr. Starnes, before long you'll be running a marathon." And then, he left.

I thought he was nuts. I weighed three hundred pounds. I had just pulled through open-heart surgery, and this guy was talking about running a marathon? I couldn't even run to the bathroom.

Every day, Alphonso came to visit and, sure enough, one step became two and two became three, and by Friday I had managed to walk to the nurses' station with Alphonso by my side. "We're training for a marathon," he told one of my visitors. "One step at a time."

When I got back to my room, I couldn't help but think about Alphonso's declaration. It was truly absurd. I could barely walk, much less run a marathon. I laughed at the notion as I drifted off to sleep. *What a crazy idea*, I thought. And then, I had an encounter with God. For the sake of full disclosure, I'm a Baptist and I was on drugs. We typically don't have epiphanies. But I had one in my sleep. I received a divine revelation.

I've always thought the voice of God would sound a lot like James Earl Jones uttering divine wisdom with a deep, baritone vibrato. "Thou shalt run a marathon." That's what the voice said. But the voice didn't sound like James Earl Jones. And it wasn't anything all that audible. There weren't any angelic choirs. There wasn't a glowing light shining down from the heavens. But I did sense the presence of God telling me that I was going to run. Yeah, I know, it sounds crazy—and I *was* on drugs. But I truly believe I had an encounter with God that night.

At the time, I'm not sure I actually believed what I was thinking. The only thing of substance I'd ever accomplished up to now was surviving open-heart surgery. And I came from a long line of people who were not exactly specimens of athletic prowess.

"There's only one reason you should ever run," Dad told me one day. "And that's if someone or something very large and hairy is chasing you." It made perfect sense.

The very idea that I could even walk, much less run, was absurd. I could barely get out of bed. I was hooked up to more machines than I could count. And my athletic résumé was paper-thin. I may have been the only child in the nation to get cut from his T-ball team. I was a really, really, really bad athlete. *Really.* I was so bad my high school physical education teacher nicknamed me "Cool Breeze"—as in, every time I went to bat that's the only thing that was generated: a cool breeze.

But isn't God in the business of using the most unsuspecting people to accomplish His will? I'm sure there were plenty of great orators roaming around Egypt, but God decided to use a guy with a stutter to lead His people to the Promised Land. And you just know there had to be some big, beefy guys who could've put Goliath in his place, but God chose to use a scrawny shepherd boy.

As I was contemplating the covenant I was about to make with God, I was reminded of a wonderful song by Ron Kenoly called "Use Me."

I was a poster child for the "least of these." My life was in need of an extreme physical makeover. I needed a new song in my life, a new direction. And for now, God was pointing me in the direction of the impossible. But if we believe and we trust, God can make the impossible possible. *I can do all things through Christ who strengthens me.* Isn't that what the apostle Paul wrote in Philippians 4:13? The key is not just believing and trusting, but acting on that belief and trust.

And so, on a warm summer night, on the fourth floor of Sutter Memorial Hospital, I decided to let go and let God take control. *If You can use anything, You can use me,* I prayed. *Just don't make me wear those skimpy running shorts.*

12

THE NURSE, THE WARM TOWEL, AND THE HAIRCUT

Normally, I'm a pretty nice guy. Happy-go-lucky is how some people have described me. But when I get sick, I transform into a very ornery person. I can't help it. It's genetic. Dad was like that. So was my grandfather. One sniffle and I'm off to bed with a laundry list of demands—chicken noodle soup, Nutter Butters, and the remote control. So you might imagine that after my heart surgery, I had a bit of an attitude. Actually, it was the mother of all pity parties, and heaven help the folks who got an invitation.

In spite of my ornery behavior, I found the following passage of Old Testament Scripture to be more than true: "The Lord is gracious and full of compassion, slow to anger and great in mercy. The Lord is good to all, and His tender mercies are over all His works" (Ps. 145:8-9).

Isn't it peculiar that the King of kings, the Lord of lords, the Maker of the heavens and the earth, lavishes us with *tender* mercies? I've always wondered why the psalm writer would use such a word to describe the Lord's loving-kindness. During my hospitalization, I believe I may have found the answer.

"Are we having a bad day?"

The question caught me slightly off guard. We *are not having a bad day*, I thought to myself. I *am having a bad day*. The nurse was just trying to make small talk, but I was not in the mood. I was in a great deal of pain, and for whatever reason the medicine coursing through my body was not working. I grumbled to my nurse, but she ignored my nasty attitude.

"Is that a Bible on your nightstand?" she asked. Well, obviously it was. What in the world was this lady's problem? "You know, we're not really supposed to talk about religion, but you might want to check out God's 911 call." I suppose the confused look on my face was pretty apparent. "Psalm 91, verse 1," she said. "You might want to read it." And then, she left.

Oh, boy! Another test—and I blew it. The nurse was just trying to be nice, and I was a complete jerk. I had no one to blame but myself—not even the drugs could get me out of this one. I stared at my Bible for the longest time before

I had the guts to pick it up and thumb over to Psalm 91:1. When I did, here's what I found: "He who dwells in the secret place of the Most High shall abide under the shadow of the Almighty." There it was in black and white. God's answer to our cry for help—His 911 call.

I always liked that word *secret.* When I was a little boy, I had a secret place—a mulberry bush that grew just outside my bedroom window. I was small enough to crawl inside, the thick branches providing the perfect camouflage for my hiding place. It was the ideal place to sneak away from the worries of the world and read a comic book or sort my baseball card collection. Isn't that how God is? For those of us who believe, He is our refuge in times of distress and pain. As the psalm writer exalts, "I will say of the Lord, 'He is my refuge and my fortress; my God, in Him I will trust'" (v. 2). And, as I came to discover, He was *my* refuge in Room 419 of Sutter Memorial Hospital.

I met Velma during my first night on the cardiac floor. She grew up in one of the Baltic States and had a wonderful Eastern European accent. Velma worked the late shift and was responsible for waking me up so I could be administered medicine to make me sleep— or something like that. And on occasion, she would slip me something sweet to eat—always Jell-O, never a Nutter Butter (I love Nutter Butters!).

Honestly, I found it hard to sleep. The pain in my chest was particularly bad at night, but I refused to take morphine because I was terrified of getting addicted. So Velma came up with a rather unorthodox treatment. She came into my room holding a thick white towel—the kind you might find at a fancy hotel. It was steaming hot. She had heated the towel in a microwave oven. She gently placed it over my chest. "This should help ease the pain," she said. "Now you close your eyes and sleep."

And, you know something? It worked like a charm. The following night, she came bearing fresh towels and a gentle smile. "Is there anything else you need?" she asked.

"How about some Nutter Butters?" I asked.

"Don't push it," she said.

I'm a vain person. There. I said it. Todd Starnes, albeit rotund, is vain. The source of my vanity is my hair. I can't help it if I was blessed with a good head of hair. Those golden-blonde locks have served me well over the years, surviving the feathered look of the eighties and an unfortunate incident involving a perm in the early nineties. Unfortunately, my hair would not survive my brush with death.

After I was weaned from the ventilator, I began complaining to anyone who would listen that my hair needed to be washed. I know there were a multitude of things I could've complained about (say the gaping hole in my chest), but I was honestly worried about my greasy hair. At one point, the ICU nursing staff was taking bets on whether to put me back on the ventilator—just to get me to shut up!

What happened next is the subject of much debate, but let me say in my defense that I was heavily medicated. I apparently began flirting with two rather attractive nurses. The conversation somehow led to a suggestion that they cut my hair, which they did. In retrospect, that was a very, very bad idea.

A few days later the Laings dropped by for a visit. I could tell from the looks on their faces something was wrong. "Oh, my gosh," said John Paul. "What happened to your hair?" His mother admonished him, but it was too late.

"What do you mean?" I reached up to touch my hair. Instead, it came out! "Sweet mercy," I exclaimed. "I'm losing my hair!" I rang the emergency call button, demanding to speak to my cardiologist. It seems the nurses had just about shaved all the hair from my head. And, whatever patches were left were falling out.

John Paul chimed in, "How about a hairpiece?" I was clearly not amused.

My doctor listened intently to my concerns. "It's not unusual for patients to experience hair loss after a major surgery," he said. "Sometimes the hair loss is exacerbated by worry. So my suggestion is not to worry about it."

That's it? That's the advice? Not to worry? How am I not supposed to worry about going bald? And for that matter, now I'm worried about being worried about going bald. And for that matter, it wasn't the surgery that caused my hair to fall out; it was the botched ICU haircut—the one I signed off on (while I was heavily medicated, I might add). I told the doctor I needed another blood pressure pill. On second thought, I suggested he'd better make it a double.

What's the point of surviving heart surgery if you have to go through the rest of your life looking like Howie Mandel? No offense to Howie Mandel, of course. I was Samson—done in by a pair of nursing-school Delilahs.

Later that night, there was a knock at my hospital door. It was my pastor, Dr. Reed, and his wife, Brenda. I couldn't fathom what my pastor was doing at the hospital, especially at that late hour. When he wasn't tending his First Baptist Church flock, Dr. Reed was consumed with the lives of his four children. I've never met such a busy man. Yet, here he was, well after visiting hours—in my hospital room.

"What are you doing here?" I asked.

"Well, I'm here to do something about that mess on top of your head," he replied. Not exactly the words of spiritual encouragement I was expecting to hear, but he certainly had my attention. "I'm here to give you a haircut."

Now I know that men of the cloth can marry people, baptize people, and even bury them. But this was the first recollection I had of a barbershop preacher. And for some strange reason, I thought it unseemly that a pastor would stoop to such a thing. "But you're a preacher," I protested. "You shouldn't be doing something like this. You are a minister."

Dr. Reed was not moved. He ignored my protestations and helped me from my bed and into a chair. The pastor promptly whipped out an array of scissors and combs, his wife gripped a broom, and I sat dumbfounded in that chair— partly bewildered and partly amazed.

Then, the Holy Spirit brought to mind a wonderful passage of Scripture from the Gospel of John.

> After that, He poured water into a basin and began to wash the disciples' feet, and to wipe them with the towel with which He was girded. Then He came to Simon Peter. And Peter said to Him, "Lord, are You washing my feet?" Jesus answered and said to him, "What I am doing you do not understand now, but you will know after this" (13:5-7).

In the case of my pastor, sometimes the shepherd must shear the flock. I was a bit overwhelmed and incredibly touched by this simple act of kindness. Sadly, we live in a world of supersized churches and preachers with supersized egos—where the pastoral duties are relegated to underlings. I realized how blessed I was to have a pastor who went the extra mile, who set aside his own comfort to minister to one of his flock. In the quiet of the night, I watched my pastor use a pair of scissors to demonstrate God's unconditional and sacrificial love.

A few months later I was invited to share my testimony during a Sunday morning church service, and I recounted the story about the pastor's late-night visit.

Afterward, Dr. Reed stood in the pulpit and told the congregation how he learned to cut hair. "It was part of my chores on the family farm," he said. "My job was to shave the pigs."

13

BREAKING WIND
AND
OTHER LESSONS
IN HUMILITY

A few of the church kids came by my hospital room to cheer me up.

"You're going bald," one of them said before the whole group launched into a rousing version of the VeggieTales song "Oh, Where Is My Hairbrush?" They especially enjoyed the verse that goes, "No hair for my hairbrush." I smiled and let out an obligatory courtesy chuckle before reminding them about the story of Elisha.

A group of teenagers surrounded the prophet near Bethel and started making fun of his bald head. Elisha was apparently having a bad hair day. So he cursed the boys in the name of the Lord, and two bears came down and ate every last one of them (2 Kings 2:23-24).

The church kids stopped laughing. Must have been something I said.

By nature, I'm a very private and discreet person. I'm not given to loud outbursts or being the life of the party. I'm fairly content to sit and enjoy the conversation of others. That's one of the reasons I chose the radio side of broadcast journalism. You can talk with millions of people without them staring back.

I barely uttered a word during my entire high school experience. I was content with being the editor of the school newspaper—a bona fide geek. In ninth grade, I tried to shed my status as a nerd by auditioning for the school production of *West Side Story*. I wanted to be a member of the Jets— staging imaginary fights with the Sharks and dancing with good-looking girls. As it turns out, one of the cast members is a geeky gang-member wannabe. He sits around the candy store reading comic books. I want you to take a wild guess as to which role I was assigned. I was typecast even in the school play!

I was painfully shy. I'm not quite sure why— that's just who I was. And to a large extent, my proclivity to being private followed me into adulthood. All that changed, though, when I had my surgery.

When you have major surgery, your life becomes an open book. My team of doctors wanted to know every single thing about me.

"Do you drink?"

"No."

"Do you smoke?"

"No."

"Sexually promiscuous?"

"No."

My doctor stopped, put down his pen, and peered across his bifocals. "What are you—a Mormon or something?"

"Actually, I'm a Baptist."

"Oh. Interesting."

And he wanted to know other things—like what I ate, what I drank. "And what can you tell me about your movements, Mr. Starnes?"

I thought for a moment before telling the doctor that I enjoyed portions of Bach and Beethoven, but did not have a particularly favorite movement. It seems, though, that the doctor was not referring to musical notes.

And that brings me to what is possibly the most humiliating moment of this journey. I'm sure there's some multisyllabic term for what I'm about to share, but I'm going to keep it simple.

When I had open-heart surgery, the surgeon stopped my heart. I was hooked to a heart-lung machine that kept me alive—albeit artificially—while they transplanted the new heart valve. Basically, they turned off my body, and when that happens, it takes a while for your system to reboot. First, I started breathing on my own. Then, I was able to start ingesting food. But the clear sign I was on the road to recovery came when my—well, how shall I put this—my engine began to backfire.

(If you are eating a snack right now, you might want to skip over this part.)

It happened while a group of church friends was visiting. Tom and Jeannine were there, and

I believe Pastor Wayne and Nancy were as well. We were having a pleasant conversation when all of a sudden I felt a rumble in my tummy.

That doesn't feel quite right, I thought. *And all they've been feeding me is Jell-O. Hmm. . . .*

And then, it happened again. I asked Pastor Wayne to call a nurse, who promptly arrived just as the first gust of wind evacuated my body. And then—another.

I was mortified! I had just broken wind in front of the music minister and the head of the Woman's Missionary Union. I could tell from the looks on their faces that we were all in unfamiliar etiquette territory.

Pastor Wayne attempted to bring some civility to the moment. "Perhaps we should pray...." That was about as far as he got before doubling over in laughter. And then it happened again—generating more laughter and a look of relief from the floor nurse.

"Oh, this is wonderful news," she exclaimed. "Todd is passing gas!"

The nurse announced to anyone within earshot that my system was rebooting—apparently with great gusto. I was well on my way to recovery. There I was, one of the most discreet people on the planet, farting uncontrollably in front of my church leaders. I could just imagine the praise report in the church newsletter:

PRAISE REPORT! BROTHER TODD
IS FINALLY BREAKING WIND!

I'm not quite sure how much methane was released into the atmosphere on that day, but it's safe to say the ozone layer took a pretty big hit, as did my ego.

If I could have, I would've unplugged the machines in my hospital room and let nature take its course. My friends, of course, were unrelenting in their good-natured teasing, and they have deemed the day I started passing gas as one of the funniest stories of the year.

Yeah. It was a real gas!

14

GOING HOME

I spent eight days in Sutter Medical Center, room 457. The surgery had been a great success. I had grown especially close to the nurses who cared for me. These men and women are on the front lines of the battle to heal broken bodies and wounded spirits. They were gentle and kind, but when they needed to be, they could be unbending taskmasters. Their job was to poke and prod me out of the bed—to teach me how to start living again.

Those eight days were so difficult. I had somehow managed to survive open-heart surgery, but I wasn't sure what kind of life awaited me on the other side. I was someone who thrived on independence. Now, I could hardly walk a few steps without assistance.

Still, after eight days, it was time to go home. Initially, I was overjoyed—even though I would not be returning to my apartment. I would be living with Pastor Wayne and Nancy. And a host of church ladies had already signed up to provide me with the best home cooking this side of heaven. In a way, I was ready to go—until it was actually time to leave.

An orderly wheeled me to the front of the hospital. To this day, I remember how bright the sky was and how warm the sun felt when it hit my face. And, for a brief moment, I hesitated.

I can't do this. I can't leave this place. How am I going to make it?

I was suddenly overwhelmed with doubt. I didn't want to leave. I didn't want to get out of the wheelchair. So many people had been taking care of me, but now it was time to take care of myself. I wasn't sure if I was up for the task.

I should've recognized it as a spiritual attack. In our weakest moments, Satan will try to exploit our circumstances—making us feel sorry for ourselves and questioning our relationship with Christ.

A great truth is found in the Casting Crowns song "Who Am I?" The answer, of course, is that I am a child of God. The One who made the universe also made me. He knows my name. He knows my hurt. And He promised to never leave me, to always be there for me. And He was there on May 26, 2005, as I sat in a wheelchair contemplating my predicament.

"Be strong and courageous" is the command God gave to Joshua. And it's the same command He gives to Christians today. It was the command He gave me outside Sutter Memorial Hospital.

Be strong and courageous, Todd. Be strong and courageous.

I felt Nancy take my hand. She gave me a gentle squeeze. "It's okay, Todd. You can do this."

She was right. I could do this. And with a bit of prodding I stood up, walked to the car, and left Sutter Memorial Hospital with a profound sense of gratitude. The journey of a thousand miles had begun.

15

ON MY OWN

I awoke in a cold sweat. The noise was pushing me closer to the edge of insanity. No matter what I tried, it would just not go away. It was my heart valve. The clicking kept getting louder and louder.

The noise is caused by the valve doors opening and closing as blood moves through the heart. It creates a sound very similar to the ticking of a clock. It was nearly impossible to sleep, and whenever I did get some rest, I woke up expecting to see Morley Safer from *60 Minutes* hovering near my bed.

"It takes some time to get used to," my cardiologist said. "In a few months you won't even give it a second thought."

A few months? I wasn't interested in a few months. I wanted instant gratification.

"Look at the bright side," he said. "At least you know it's working."

Thank you, Dr. House.

So he sent me on my way with a bottle of sleeping pills and a warning not to get addicted. The last thing I needed was a weeklong vacation at the Betty Ford Clinic.

The adjustment was difficult—living at home, that is. I would fall asleep clutching my cell phone. I figured if something happened, I could call for help. I even programmed 911 into my speed dial.

Life became fairly regimented. I got up around eight o'clock and ate breakfast. The Krispy Kreme doughnuts were gone. Jeannine bought me a year's supply of heart-healthy cereal. Even if I closed my eyes and wished really hard, it still tasted like tree bark.

I took two walks every day—one in the morning, the other in the afternoon. Lunch was at noon, followed by my one treat of the day—a Baptist Martini. For you Lutherans out there, that's a Diet Coke. I pretty much spent the rest of the day watching Dr. Phil and Judge Judy while listening to the rhythmic clicking of my valve. I felt like I was trapped in the cardiac wing of Gitmo.

The highlight of my social calendar was Friday. That's when I visited my heart doctor. My blood was tested once a week. I was taking blood thinners. It's the one drawback to my mechanical heart valve. If my blood gets too thick, it could form a clot on the new valve. That would be unpleasant. So I take blood thinners every day. And I have to watch my diet. Too much iron and it'll throw off my Coumadin levels.

My first visit did not go so well. On paper, the Coumadin test isn't so bad. The nurse pricks my finger with a tiny needle, draws a small amount of blood, and slaps on a bandage. Unfortunately, I have a problem with needles. As soon as she poked me, I passed out. I fell right out on the floor. It was quite a scene. The next week, it happened again.

During my third visit, the nurse closed the door and gave me a stern look. "Mr. Starnes. I'm having a difficult day, so if you plan on passing out you'd better tell me now." Would you believe I stayed upright? Who says tough love doesn't work? After my test, she even treated me to a lollipop.

I was in a foul mood—and it wasn't going away. I'd been snapping at everyone about everything. I was an unpleasant person to be around. I didn't even want to be around me. I told my cardiologist.

"That's normal," he said. "Most heart patients have mood swings after their surgery. Your body has been through a very serious ordeal. It takes some time."

107

That was a relief. I had been pretty moody. One day I was watching a Mrs. Butterworth commercial when I suddenly broke into tears.

"You should consider counseling."

"I just wanted pancakes," I said. "Wait a minute. Do you think I'm nuts?"

"Therapists can help you get your head around what's happened to you physically and mentally. You need to really consider doing this, Todd. Depression after heart surgery is a very real thing."

I rejected his offer without even giving it a second thought. There was absolutely no way I was going to see a therapist.

"I'm not depressed!" I shouted. "I just missed Mrs. Butterworth."

He scribbled the name of a therapist on a sheet of paper and pushed it across his desk. I pushed it right back.

"You are incorrigible," he said. "And stay away from the pancakes."

"You need to relax," said one of my colleagues at KFBK. "Go out and have a drink."

I figured it couldn't hurt, so I walked over to The Streets of London, a British pub in midtown Sacramento, and bellied up to the bar.

"Looks like you've had a rough day, partner. How about a little hair from the dog that bit ya?"

"Give me a Baptist Martini," I said. "And, you'd better make it a double."

16

A Blessing Denied

Dad hated to ask for directions. And that was a tragedy on many levels—mostly because my dad did not have a sense of direction.

One summer, the family piled into our bright-blue Oldsmobile and set off from our home in Mississippi to the Ozark Mountains. By the time we got to Dallas, Mom suggested that Dad stop and ask someone for directions. Dad stubbornly refused to give in—suggesting instead that Dallas was the southernmost city in the Ozarks.

Even though I was ten years old, I had already started to develop the investigative skills that would later propel me into journalism. I asked what I thought was an obvious question: "So where are the mountains?"

I was grounded.

Men do not fail—so to admit failure is not an option. It's an irrational argument, but one that many men live and die by. I was one of those guys.

We're the kind of men who are self-sufficient. We have all the answers. We don't need anyone else's help. We're the ones who are always there to help others. Ladies, it's a guy thing. We don't expect you to understand.

So when my doctor told me I was going to need around-the-clock help when I was sent home from the hospital, I laughed.

"That's okay," I told him. "I think I can handle it myself."

My doctor didn't exactly tell me I was nuts, but I knew he was thinking it. "You don't seem to understand. You won't be able to drive a car for about a month. You are going to be in quite a bit of pain. You won't even be able to lift your arms above your head to change a lightbulb."

My nearest relatives were three time zones away, I was single, and I wasn't about to ask anyone at church for help. And it didn't have anything to do with being a guy. It had everything to do with pride. I had convinced myself that I could take care of myself. I wish I could blame my flawed rationale on the drugs, but I came up with that brilliant idea stone-sober.

A few days before surgery I got a telephone call from Pastor Wayne and his wife, Nancy, inviting me to their home for dinner.

"I can't," I said. "I'm going to Wal-Mart."

"Why are you going to Wal-Mart?"

"I need lightbulbs."

I explained to Pastor Wayne that once I had surgery I wouldn't be able to change any lightbulbs.

So I was planning on replacing the old bulbs with fresh bulbs so I could convalesce in bright light.

Pastor Wayne thought I was nuts. "Nancy and I have already spoken with your parents, and we've all agreed that you are going to come to our home after your surgery."

I was more than a bit irritated. I couldn't believe my folks would go behind my back. I was perfectly capable of taking care of myself and told Pastor Wayne thanks, but no thanks.

"I'm sorry," he said in a very reverent voice. "You assumed you had a choice. You will be coming to stay with us, and that's that."

A few years ago, a member of our church became sick and a group of us volunteered to deliver meals to his family. I remember the joy that filled my heart and the blessing I received as I reached out to help this brother in Christ. Unfortunately, I was about to deny my own church family a blessing all because of my foolish pride.

The apostle Paul admonishes us in Galatians 6:2 to "bear one another's burdens." In doing so, we receive a spiritual blessing.

In Hebrews 10:24-25 Paul goes a step further: "And let us consider one another in order to stir up love and good works, not forsaking the assembling of ourselves together, as is the manner of some, but exhorting one another, and so much the more as you see the Day approaching."

I was learning that Christians don't have to go it alone. On the contrary, we are supposed to look after each other. We're supposed to spur one another on to good deeds. We are supposed to help each other. That's why being a part of a church is so important. We hear our pastors tell us about building community and fellowship. There's a reason for that. My revelation came about two days before I left the hospital.

I was in quite a bit of pain, and there were large bandages on my chest and stomach. I was aching from my head to my toes. My physical therapy was progressing, but I didn't have much strength. A trip to the bathroom resulted in a half-hour nap. My doctor was right. I couldn't lift my arms above my chest. I was alive, but I was far from self-sufficient. My discovery came just before Pastor Wayne and Nancy dropped by for a visit.

"I don't think I can do this," I told them. "If the offer still stands, I'd like to come and stay with you guys."

Pastor Wayne smiled and said, "As if you ever had a choice."

Over the coming weeks, I would be lavished with food, gifts, and much love from my church family. I don't believe I will ever be able to repay them for their wonderful acts of kindness. And to think that I almost denied them the blessing of serving a fellow believer in need!

I sure am glad that the Lord loves us in spite of ourselves.

17

THE CLOCK
IS TICKING

I have a sneaking suspicion my family wants me to get married. Aunt Norma said as much one day, "When are you going to settle down?" At my age, it's a fair question. And, trust me, I've fielded a lot of questions. Let's just say that when it comes to dating, I've been most unfortunate.

As frustrating as it's been for the aunts and uncles and cousins, you can imagine it's been pretty frustrating for me. Once you get over the agony and humiliation that comes with rejection, dating is not all that bad.

Several of my church friends have given me counsel on my dating life—the chief problem being that I don't have a dating life.

"Maybe you've set your standards too high," said one friend, trying to offer some encouragement. Right now my only standard involves not being dead—so I don't think that's the problem.

"Maybe they've set *their* standards too high," another church member countered.

Another chimed in, "You know, Todd. It's not what's on the outside that counts. The true beauty of a person is what's on the inside." That very well may be the case, but let's be honest, ladies. Given the choice, would you rather go out for a night on the town with Brad Pitt or a three-hundred-pound guy with a heart condition? I rest my case.

Dating is like playing a football game. It takes a game plan to make it into the end zone. Unfortunately, I'm the Detroit Lions of the professional dating world. I've been sitting on the bench for so long, I'm not sure I would know what to do once I got called into the game.

A few months after my surgery, several of the ladies at KFBK suggested I get into the game. At that point, I'd lost about forty pounds and was beginning to develop a little self-confidence. "Besides," said one of my colleagues, "you have a brand-new heart valve. You need to take it out for a spin." After a generous amount of prodding, I relented and decided to give it a shot.

The object of my affection was an amazingly beautiful and kind girl who worked at a coffee-house near my apartment. She was always friend-ly, and it turned out she was also a Christian. And when it came to making coffee, she really knew how to put the froth on my latte. The hard part was figuring out how to invite her to dinner. The first effort resulted in total failure. I worked myself up into such a frenzy I had to take a nitroglycerin tablet. I regrouped and, the next morning, I found the courage to invite her to dinner. When she accepted my invitation, I walked outside, slumped onto a park bench, and popped another nitroglycerin tablet. "Sweet mercy," I said. "Dating is awesome, but it's going to kill me."

The date was going according to plan. We ate dinner at Spataro, an incredible restaurant in downtown Sacramento, took in a movie at the downtown IMAX, and ended our night with a stroll through the gardens around the state capitol. As we settled into a park bench to enjoy the star-filled night, I pulled the old "reach-out-your-arms-like-you're-stretching" move. It worked like a charm. She put her head on my shoulder, and I put my arm around her. And then—it happened.

"Todd," she asked, "do you hear that?"

"Hear what?"

"That noise?"

"What kind of noise?"

"I don't know. It's weird. It sounds like a clock—a ticking clock."

The color drained from my face. It was my heart valve, and sure enough, it was really ticking. I had failed to mention to my date that I was recovering from heart surgery. It was a strategic decision. I'm a dating novice, but I'm pretty sure women aren't all that interested in dating guys with gaping chest wounds.

"A ticking sound?"

"Yeah. Like a really loud clock."

"It may be my watch. It's new, you know."

I'm not too sure she bought my excuse.

"If that's the case you may want to take it back," she said.

"Why's that?"

"It's ticking faster."

Stupid heart valve.

I'm lonely.

I have the most wonderful family in the world. I'm blessed with faithful friends. And yet, I can't shake this feeling of loneliness. I've often wondered why I'm still single. I try not to think about it, but I do. The other day, I was jogging through the park and watched as a guy played football with his little boy. I saw young couples walking hand in hand. It seemed as though every twist and turn I took revealed an undeniable truth: I am still single.

When I was in high school, I was voted "Most Likely to Be Ward Cleaver." I was the kid everyone else thought would be the picture-perfect dad. The irony being that I'm just about the only person in my graduating class who is not married. I've often asked God about my dilemma. Unfortunately, God doesn't keep track of time on my watch. And, as of this writing, He has yet to reveal His betrothal plans for me.

But I do know this—He is faithful and He is a just God, and He desires that His children be happy. One day God will reveal the future Mrs.

Starnes. And I know she will be someone who is passionately in love with the Lord, someone who loves children, and someone who will love me—unconditionally—ticking heart valve and all.

18

GO EAST, YOUNG MAN!

Rush Limbaugh called Sacramento his adopted hometown. I can understand why. I absolutely love that city. The climate is amazingly livable, it's about an hour's drive from Tahoe, Yosemite, and San Francisco—and it has a lot of trees. Someone once told me it reminded them of Paris.

I lived in a small apartment in midtown. I walked to the grocery store, ate dinner at outdoor cafés, and took my evening walks around the state capitol building.

But I think what makes Sacramento so wonderful are her people. It's a really friendly city, and it's probably the most normal California city. Fortunately, most of the nut-jobs and granola crowd settled around the Bay Area—leaving Sacramento to be a good family town. It sort of had a Southern feel, although their idea of barbecue is to throw a few burgers and hot dogs on the grill. But even that's forgivable!

And I especially loved my job. KFBK is one of the great heritage radio stations in the nation. I never thought in a million years I'd have a chance to work there. But there I was—working in the same studio where Rush once worked, holding the microphone that his formerly nicotine-stained fingers once held, doing that "excellence in broadcasting" thing. I was a radio "ditto head."

I'm the kind of reporter who likes to go where the action is. When it comes to my job, I'm a risk taker. I'd trudge through a blizzard for the sake of a good story. One time, I got so close to a wildfire my shoes partially melted. I believe they are still on display in KFBK's makeshift museum. So, you can imagine the trauma I was going through post-surgery. I was chomping at the bit to get back to work. About two months after my surgery, my cardiologist gave me the thumbs-up to return. Imagine my surprise and delight when a big story hit our city. We had an outbreak of tornadoes.

Back in the South, tornadoes are a big deal, but we're used to them. It's sort of like Britney Spears falling off the wagon. We know it's going to happen, we just don't know when. But tornadoes in Sacramento were a rarity. As soon as the first weather bulletin sounded, I jumped into a news Jeep and flew into action.

Sacramento's landscape is breathtaking. The east is the Delta, miles and miles of flat land similar to Mississippi's Delta. To the north and west are the snowcapped Sierra Mountains. On a clear day, you can see the mountains. It was perfect terrain to spot twisters dropping from the sky. I slammed on the accelerator and flew along Interstate 5 as dark storm clouds gathered on the horizon.

Traffic was slowing down to a crawl, and some people actually pulled onto the emergency lane to watch the incredible scene unfold.

These people are crazy. Don't they know a tornado is coming? They need to be taking shelter.

Of course, I needed to heed my own advice, but there was a story to cover. Besides, I had survived open-heart surgery. So what's the big deal with a tornado?

I was on the outskirts of Sacramento heading north when I saw two fire engines and a battalion chief's car parked on an overpass near ARCO Arena, where the Sacramento Kings play professional basketball. I pulled off the interstate, parked my Jeep, and grabbed my gear.

I asked the chief, "What are you guys doing on top of the bridge?"

"We're waiting for the twister to get here," he said.

"I don't mean to question your strategy, but shouldn't we be under the bridge?"

He didn't have time to answer because the civil defense sirens began wailing and, as we stood on the overpass, our jaws dropped as the sky opened and a funnel cloud came rotating from the clouds. I thought my ticker was about to explode.

"We've got rotation," I shouted into my micro-phone, alerting my producer that we needed to go live. And within minutes, KFBK's 50,000-watt signal was broadcasting my tornado play-by-play to most of Northern California. The funnel cloud became a tornado. It touched down about a mile due north of the overpass and caused quite a bit of damage. Fortunately, no one was hurt.

Tornadoes in the South and Midwest are nasty devils. They are violent and deadly monsters. The tornadoes that touched down in Sacramento were uniquely Californian in shape and manner.

Our afternoon news anchors, Kitty O'Neal and Jay Alan, asked me to describe what I was seeing. "Kitty, these are the most unusual funnel clouds I've seen. There are three, very slender, moving gracefully across the Delta, sashaying from one side to the other—almost as if they are dancing."

Between you and me, those were the most effeminate tornadoes I've ever seen.

Working at KFBK was just a lot of fun, and I imagined myself having a very long and happy career in Northern California. My post-surgery life was beginning to take shape, and I could see why God had brought me to Sacramento. I had wonderful friends, a tremendous church family, and had finally grown accustomed to 114-degree summers (it's a dry heat, you know). I was, in a word, content.

Then one day, out of the blue, I received a telephone call from Mitch Davis, the vice president of news at Fox News Radio in New York. "We've heard your stuff," he told me. "And we'd like to fly you out here for a few days."

I talked it over with my bosses at KFBK, and they agreed that I should at the very least enjoy a free trip to New York. I also checked with my cardiologist. He was a bit more cautious. It would be a long trip, he said, and he wasn't sure if I was up for the rigors of the journey. But there was a part of me that wanted to go—that needed to go—so I threw caution to the wind, accepted the free ticket from Fox News, and headed due east.

I hadn't been in New York since the terrorist attacks. I had forgotten how insane that place is—all those people, most of whom don't speak English, trying to get to the same place at the same time. It was chaos. And September in New York is not exactly the best time to visit. As soon as I stepped off the plane, I gasped for air. It was incredibly humid.

Am I really willing to give up Northern California for this?

I took a cab from the airport and got settled in a charming boutique hotel just a few blocks from Fox News. It was one of those feng shui hotels. I didn't know whether to eat my bed or sleep on it. I'm a Motel 6 kind of guy, and I was definitely out of my element.

My cardiologist had been right. I was physically exhausted and quickly fell asleep. The next morning, I wasn't much better. The humid air was making it difficult for me to breathe, and my chest was beginning to hurt. Nevertheless, I dressed and walked across Sixth Avenue to the Fox News Corner of the World. That corner is at

Sixth Avenue and Forty-seventh Street. I remember standing on the plaza, staring into the air. The tower seemed to disappear into the clouds.

Boy, I am definitely out of my element.

I shook my head, laughed, and walked inside. A security guard asked for my identification. "Oh yes, Mr. Starnes. We've been waiting for you." Within a few minutes someone escorted me upstairs to the fifteenth floor where the radio news operation is based.

The day was filled with all sorts of interviews and tours. It was a whirlwind event. All the while, I found it hard to believe I was actually in the Fox News building. I'd been a huge fan of Fox News Channel from the first day of its existence. I believed in their mission and purpose— to present the news in a fair and balanced way. Never in a million years would I have imagined myself getting a tour of the building, much less working there.

There was nothing remarkable about that day. I plodded through the interviews and tried to look more energetic than I was. At one point, the pain was so intense I began to perspire.

It was not my greatest moment. I left New York later that afternoon destined for California. I really didn't have a good feeling about how things had gone, but I was still content.

At least I got to see New York, eat at the Carnegie Deli, and visit Fox News. It'll be nice to get back home. And, on the plus side, California doesn't have humidity.

When I got back home, my cardiologist ordered me to bed. "You need to rest," he said. "That trip was not a good thing."

But it was the network, I told him. And when the network calls—you go.

For a few weeks, my life was upended. I hadn't heard anything from New York, and the folks at KFBK were pushing me for information. My family had launched a prayer-athon. I was trying to figure out what God was doing. I was happy in Sacramento. My health was precarious. My finances had been depleted. This was the worst possible time for a move.

But, as I've discovered, God's timing is not exactly our timing. A few days later, I received a telephone call in the newsroom. It was Mitch Davis, from Fox News.

"This is the call you've been waiting for," he said. "I'd like to offer you a job at Fox News Radio."

I left Sacramento with mixed feelings. Friends and colleagues gathered to say goodbye at my favorite restaurant, Spataro. As I took in the scene that night, I realized the blessings God had lavished on my life—a good job, good friends, and good meatballs (you should really try the meatballs at Spataro).

I packed up my Ford Taurus and headed due east, bidding a fond farewell to the well-tanned and body-sculpted state of California. I was somewhere in New Mexico when I began feeling a bit sad.

Boy, I sure could use a good dose of comfort.

And a few miles down the road, my prayer was answered. There was a larger-than-life sign on Interstate 40: CRACKER BARREL—NEXT EXIT.

19

New York, New York, a Heck of a Town!

I love New York City—the bright lights, the hustle and bustle. I love the way lower Manhattan looks from the middle of the Brooklyn Bridge. I love the way pizza tastes at Lombardi's in Little Italy. I love the way Central Park smells on a sunny spring day. Yep. This city fits me like a glove.

But like people from every other part of the fruited plain, New Yorkers have their foibles. Take, for example, taxicab drivers who don't speak English. My Aunt Sue took an unfortunate ride in a taxi with a driver who hailed from one of the Balkan States and apparently thought he was competing in a NASCAR race. It was an unpleasant experience for all of us.

But this town also gets a bad rap. For instance, the idea that New Yorkers are rude is an urban legend. They're just in a hurry to get someplace.

It's true that they enjoy flavoring their language with curse words—but it's nothing personal. I've actually heard one particularly naughty word used as a noun, verb, adjective, and preposition—all in one sentence. New Yorkers are quirky people. They're sort of the hot sauce in the American melting pot. That being said, it does take some time to get used to the city.

In the South, we embrace newcomers with great gusto. We lavish them with food, personal visits, and suggestions on where to attend church. Whenever someone new moved into the neighborhood, Mom was one of their first visitors. She would arrive armed with a basket of home-baked goodies—her muffins were the best. It was the neighborly thing to do, she would always tell me. And inevitably, the very first question she would ask was, "So have you found a place to worship yet?" It's a Southern quirk—our way of finding out if the new folks are Baptists, Methodists, Lutherans, or Catholics. By the time I hit junior high school, I figured out Mom was using those muffins as bait to get folks to visit the local First Baptist Church. That woman was shrewd!

In New York, they could care less where you attend church, but when it comes to your apartment, they don't waste a moment getting into your business.

"So, how much do you pay for rent?"

Folks, New York City is a very expensive place to live. When I was apartment hunting, I joked about not being able to afford to live in Harlem.

Turns out—it wasn't a joke. I couldn't even afford to live in the Bronx! My first apartment was about the size of a closet. The refrigerator was in the bathroom. That's really not such a bad thing—especially if you are prone to getting thirsty during your morning constitutional. My first apartment cost me a grand total of seventeen hundred dollars a month! I can actually say it without crying now.

I've also gotten accustomed to traveling around on the subway. I take the Q Train and it's filled with all sorts of interesting characters. My first day on the train, I boarded a nearly empty subway car and took a seat near the conductor. Within seconds, a homeless man approached me and demanded I sit somewhere else. "You're in my living room," he told me. "Now get out." I typically make it a point not to argue with homeless guys wielding bottles of malt liquor, so I muttered an apology and asked if I could sit in his den.

The key to staying safe in New York is common sense. There are just some parts of town where you don't need to be after dark, and frankly, there are some places you don't need to be during daylight. Sadly, I lived in one of those areas. And one day, I nearly met my Maker.

It was around six in the morning and I had just finished anchoring the overnight news. I left the train station, walked under a train trestle, and turned a corner to get to my apartment. Imagine my surprise when I turned the corner and found myself standing face-to-face with a naked black lady holding a baseball bat.

Now, I've been through my fair share of life experiences, but I believe this is the first one involving a naked lady holding a baseball bat.

She let out a bone-chilling scream and I did as well. "Sweet mercy!" I shouted. She raised the baseball bat and was about to charge when I took off like a bat out of you-know-where.

I raced back to the subway station and saw a group of police officers on their radios. "Officer!" I shouted. "You won't believe this, but there's a naked black lady with a baseball bat and she's chasing me."

"We know," said the officer. "We're waiting for backup."

Within just a few seconds, the entire Yonkers Police Department had assembled along with two meter maids packing heat. The naked black lady with the bat was going down!

The folks back in the newsroom were overjoyed. "Congratulations," they said. "You've just experienced your first New York moment."

"But it was in Yonkers."

"That's what makes it even better," they said.

As you can see, living in New York City takes a bit of adjustment. So to help newcomers, I've come up with a list of things you may not know about the Big Apple. This might help soften the blow on your next visit.

1. *The tea isn't sweet.* I ordered sweet iced tea during my first day in the Big Apple. The waitress

looked at me like I was from some Third World nation.

"I don't understand. Sweet what?"

"Tea. Sweet iced tea."

"I'm not following you. You want me to do what with the tea?"

I explained the instructions for making sweet iced tea, and judging the expression on her face, I wasn't too sure she understood. A few minutes later she returned to my table with a pot of hot tea, a glass of ice, and three packets of sugar.

2. *Taxi drivers don't speak English.* A number of them also have an aversion to deodorant, but that's another story. And, even if you live in Brooklyn, your driver will somehow find a way to detour through Times Square at rush hour.

3. *Bagels are not biscuits.* Bagels are an acquired taste. The good ones have the consistency of a hockey puck. The bad ones taste like a hockey puck. One day I ordered a plain bagel at a deli on Sixth Avenue.

"Do you want me to schmear your bagel?"

"You want to do what to my bagel?"

"Do you want a schmear?"

I didn't have a clue what the guy was talking about. Back home if a guy schmears another guy, he could end up getting hurt. Apparently, though, a schmear has something to do with cream cheese. I think.

4. *Once this place thaws out, it smells.* I'm not sure why. But you might want to pack a few bottles of room deodorizer.

5. *New Yorkers don't believe there's a country beyond the Hudson River.* Don't take it personally. They have this mentality that the New York way to do things is the only way to do things. And that may very well be true, kind readers. But just remember—New York may have Broadway and thin-crust pizza, but the South knows how to barbecue a pig, and we have central heat and air.

20

THE JEW,
THE GENTILE,
AND THE OLD MAN

Back home there's a church on every street corner. In New York City, there's a Starbucks on every street corner. Don't get me wrong. The Big Apple is religious. It's just not the kind of religion I'm used to. In the South, you can throw a biscuit and hit a Baptist church. In New York City, you can throw a bagel and hit a Catholic church or a Jewish synagogue.

Finding a church home was one of my first priorities. My friend Taylor Field pastors a Southern Baptist congregation in the Lower East Side called The Graffiti Church. He's been ministering here since the 1980s. You might find this hard to believe, but there are dozens of Southern Baptist churches in the Big Apple. Most are populated by folks who've relocated from Mississippi, Texas, and Georgia. After several weeks of church shopping, I finally settled on a congregation that would meet my spiritual needs. The name of the church, oddly enough, is The Journey.

We meet in a theatre on West Thirty-fourth Street, about a block or so away from Madison Square Garden. It's a great church. The pastors are young and energetic, they teach the Bible, and they are equipping hundreds of young people to spread the gospel of Christ in our city.

My friend Lauren hosts a weekly Bible study in her apartment. That's how I met Blake. He's from Oklahoma and moved here to study art. We struck up a quick friendship, and when he found out I was training for the marathon, he readily offered to help me train. I told him I could use all the help I could get.

I also met Sarah at Lauren's Bible study. I was talking with Blake when I heard someone say "y'all." I immediately knew she was from the South by the way she turned a two-syllable word into a five-syllable word. I whirled around and was delighted to find an honest-to-goodness Southern belle. She could put Scarlett O'Hara to shame, and on top of that, Sarah is from Memphis. She drinks her tea sweet, loves barbecue, and knows how to shoot a gun. As my Uncle Jerry from Coldwater, Mississippi, says, "Any girl who has a carry-and-conceal permit is a girl worth taking home."

The other great thing about Sarah is that her family is just about as crazy as mine. I know we've probably frightened the Northern members of our Bible study group with our nonstop "my-family-is-crazier-than-yours-athons."

Let's be honest, we all have members of our families who are certifiable. And if you think you don't have any crazy folks in your family tree, there's a pretty good chance you are the crazy one. Now some folks are ashamed of their off-kilter offspring—but not Southerners. Instead of squirreling them away in the attic or a home, we're prone to putting them out on the front porch in a rocking chair. We Southerners take pride in the family fruitcakes.

I'm man enough to admit that Sarah finally bested me in the crazy-family competition. Her great-grandmother died a while back, and her dad's cousin showed up at the funeral in a Confederate soldier's uniform—with a sword. Folks, that's just plain crazy.

This city would've been a lot lonelier without Lauren's Bible study group and my church family. The point is, church is important not only for the teaching, but also for the fellowship. I don't believe that Christ expects us to walk alone. We are pilgrims on a journey together. We're supposed to encourage each other and, when necessary, admonish one another. That's what being a part of God's family is about.

My neighborhood is diverse—and I do mean diverse. We have Catholics, Protestants, Muslims, Hindus, Buddhists, and, judging from the number of *Watchtower* magazines I receive, more than our fair share of Jehovah's Witnesses. Everyone gets along just fine, although I got off to a rough start with the Hindu family over on East Eighteenth Street. I offered the husband a cheeseburger. That was unfortunate.

Every Saturday I run about ten miles. Normally, I chart out a path that takes me through Central Park in Manhattan or Prospect Park near my apartment. But one day I decided to run southwest on a course that would end at Coney Island.

I always treat myself to an unhealthy snack on Saturdays, and nothing completes a ten-mile run like a hot dog slathered in mustard. And there's only one place to get a genuine dog—Nathan's Original Hot Dog, just off the Coney Island boardwalk.

It was stifling hot, even in the early morning. Janice Dean, Fox News' "Weather Machine," forecast a high near 100 degrees, and as soon as I walked outside I broke into a sweat.

Sweet mercy! This is going to be a tough run. I'm going to have to stop for something to drink.

Finding a convenience store would not be a problem. There were plenty of mom-and-pop stores along the route. After stretching, I plugged in my earphones, turned on my iPod, and started on my way. I mostly ran along Ocean Parkway, but after a while I decided to veer into one of the neighborhoods for a change of scenery.

About twenty minutes into my run, I became thirsty. The first store I came to was closed.

That's strange. Oh, well.

I jogged down another block, and sure enough, the bodega on that street was closed. As a matter of fact, every shop on the entire block was shuttered.

What in the world is going on?

My curiosity had the best of me. I was beginning to wonder if some sort of calamity had befallen the area. About two blocks later, though, I figured out what was going on. I noticed men walking in my direction dressed in long, black overcoats. They were all sporting thick beards and wearing black, wide-brimmed hats. Long curls of hair flowed down the sides of their faces.

I had stumbled into a Hassidic Jewish community. The people who live there are modest and devout followers of their faith in God. Saturday is their Sabbath and everything comes to a halt. Hassidic Jews are not allowed to do any work on the Sabbath. For example, if you inadvertently leave a light on, it cannot be turned off until after the Sabbath.

I stopped on a street corner and tried to figure out what I was going to do. I was running on empty and needed something to drink. I was about to head back to my apartment when I felt someone grab my shoulder. I bolted around and found myself face-to-face with a Hassidic Jewish man.

"Are you a Jew?"

I was startled, not by his question, but by his presence. And my iPod was blasting Brooklyn Tabernacle Choir music into my ears, so I could barely understand what he was saying.

"I'm sorry. What did you say?"

"I said—are you a Jew?"

What an odd question.

"No. I'm a Gentile. I'm a Christian."

"Please, come with me. I need your assistance."

Now if this had happened in some areas of the city, I would've laced up my running shoes and sprinted toward the nearest police precinct. But something inside me said to follow this man in black. So, I did.

We walked about a block and the heat was just unbearable.

This guy is wearing a long, black overcoat. He's going to have a heatstroke.

Soon, we reached the front of an old apartment building. He went first, but I hesitated. I wasn't quite sure where we were or what we were going to be doing. I wasn't scared—just a bit nervous. I fumbled around in my pocket for my "mugging money" just in case. If I was about to get robbed, I would have to swap my life for ten bucks and a Starbucks gift card.

"It's okay," he said. "I need your help if you don't mind."

He opened the door, and inside the hallway was a very feeble and elderly man. He looked to be about ninety years old.

"This is my father," he said. "We were on our way to our meeting, but the heat is too much. He cannot walk."

And since Hassidic Jews can't do any manual labor on the Sabbath, this stranger was in need of my assistance.

"Would you please carry my father and place him in his wheelchair?"

Suddenly, a rush of emotions flooded my heart. I remembered a warm day in Sacramento not so long ago, when I needed help and a stranger came to my rescue.

I smiled and nodded and told him I would be honored to carry his father. It was one of the most humbling experiences of my life as I helped this elderly gentleman down the stairs and gently placed him in his wheelchair.

The younger man led the way as I pushed his father to their meetinghouse. It was about four blocks away, and no one spoke a word during the ten-minute walk. Afterward, he shook my hand and thanked me for my help.

"No," I replied. "Thank you."

My response had obviously confused him.

"It was my honor as a Christian to serve you," I said. "May God bless you."

And then we went our separate ways.

A few days later, I was recounting my experiences to a colleague at Fox News Radio. My encounter with the stranger in the long, black coat had touched me in a profound way.

"You are a Shabbat goy," my colleague said.

I've been called a lot of things, but never a Shabbat goy.

"Is that a good thing or a bad thing?"

"It's a good thing," he said. "It's the name given to people who help Jewish families or organizations on the Sabbath. You were very helpful to those men."

On the contrary, I believe they were helpful to me. I believe that God placed me on that street corner for a reason—perhaps to understand that you can be a witness for Christ without shouting at the top of your lungs. My assignment from the Holy Spirit was to display the love of Christ by offering my assistance to strangers—nothing more, nothing less.

> Though I speak with the tongues of men and of angels, but have not love, I have become sounding brass or a clanging cymbal. And though I have the gift of prophecy, and understand all mysteries and all knowledge, and though I have all faith, so that I could remove mountains, but have not love, I am nothing. . . . And now abide faith, hope, love, these three; but the greatest of these is love (1 Cor. 13:1-2, 13).

And, on a very warm summer day in Brooklyn, I believe the Lord demonstrated that lesson in love using a Hassidic Jew, a born-again Christian, and an old man.

21

MY FIRST ROAD RACE

Runners are skinny.

That was my first observation as I stood at the starting line of the American Heart Association's Wall Street Run. Exactly one year after my open-heart surgery, I was about to run my first road race.

Unfortunately, I was still overweight. I had lost one hundred twenty pounds, but I was still (ahem) well-rounded. I wasn't huge by any stretch of the imagination, but standing next to all of those bone-thin runners, I felt a bit out of place. I'm not talking about Mary-Kate Olsen skinny, but it was my impression that most of them could've used a trip to one of those "meat and three" restaurants back home. As my Uncle Jerry from Coldwater, Mississippi, would say, "Them boys need some meat on their bones."

Indeed, some of those dear folks looked like they were one meal shy of being on a Sally Struthers commercial. I wanted to stand in the middle of the racecourse with a bucket of chicken saying, "Sir, please. You need a fried chicken leg."

So, there I was—an overweight guy with a mechanical heart valve about to run a race with twelve thousand skinny people. Let's just say I stood out like a cheeseburger at a PETA meeting.

The race was sponsored by the American Heart Association, and the 3.1-mile course took us through the cavernous streets of lower Manhattan, right through the heart of Wall Street, and across the finish line at the World Financial Center. It was the perfect "first race." The course was flat, fast, and relatively easy. And since the American Heart Association was the sponsor, I figured there would be plenty of cardiologists in the race—just in case.

As the minutes ticked down to seconds, I felt a tinge of nervousness.

I sure hope I can do this.

There was a knock at my apartment door in Sacramento.

It's the crack of dawn. Who in the world would be knocking at my door at this hour?

"Hi, Todd! Are you ready to get skinny? It's time to exercise!"

Jeannine.

"Good Lord, Jeannine. What are you doing here? It's the crack of dawn."

"It's time to start your exercise program. Now put on some sneakers. We're going to go walking."

Immediately after the surgery, the doctor told Jeannine, Tom, Pastor Wayne, and Nancy that I needed to lose weight.

"Don't say another word," Jeannine told the doctor. "We're already on top of it."

While I was on life support, my friends from First Baptist Fair Oaks were plotting how to slim down my well-rounded body. Since my own parents were in poor health some two thousand miles away, the Stackses and Sommerses appointed themselves my West Coast parents. They decided to share joint custody during my recovery.

Pastor Wayne and Nancy were assigned the task of my initial recovery. During my two-week convalescence at their home, they would take me on daily walks. The walks weren't all that long. The first few days, I could barely make it around their cul-de-sac. I started getting stronger and, surprisingly, I started losing weight. By the time I returned to my apartment, I could walk the length of our local mall.

All the while, I was reminded of my physical therapist's declaration that one day I would run a marathon. *What a load of hooey*, I thought. *I can't even walk around the block without getting winded.*

So Jeannine and Nancy took personal charge of my physical fitness, and since the Sommerses only lived about a mile away, Jeannine decided to appoint herself my life coach.

143

"Let's get a move on," she said. "We have some work to do."

That's how it all started. We would walk together around downtown Sacramento and around Land Park. I remember how grueling it was. I would break into a sweat after just a few blocks. I was constantly complaining about the heat, the pain, and the exercise. But Jeannine just smiled and told me to keep walking. She was determined to help me—even if I didn't want to help myself.

One day, I decided to set out on my own. The streets in midtown are lettered. I lived on G Street. By the time I got to P Street, I realized I had gone too far. My body literally shut down and I couldn't walk a single step. I sat down on a street corner and called Jeannine.

"I'm stuck," I said.

"Where are you?"

"I'm at the corner of P Street and Twenty-third."

"Don't move. I'll be there in ten minutes."

A few minutes later a police officer strolled by. He could tell that I was in distress.

"Sir, are you okay?"

"I'm fine," I replied. "I'm just waiting for a woman to pick me up."

"Sir, I'm going to need to see some ID."

It's never a good idea to tell a police officer you're waiting for a woman to pick you up—especially if you're standing at a street corner.

Dad always told me there was no need to run unless something large and furry was chasing you. For most of my life, I lived up to his edict. I never could understand why in the world someone would purposely subject themselves to miles of torture just for the sake of a T-shirt.

But now, I was one of those people. I was wearing a red hat. The American Heart Association gave them to people who had been through some sort of heart surgery. It designated us as survivors. I think it was also a strategic way for the race organizers to figure out who might drop somewhere along the course.

Oh, gosh. I forgot to stretch. I've gotta stretch.

I could hear Blake Henry's voice in my head. "What do you mean you don't stretch? That's crazy!"

I met Blake at a Bible study. I had asked our group to pray for me as I began training for the marathon. Afterward, Blake came over and introduced himself. It turned out, he was a runner and volunteered to help me train. I've always believed in God's provision, and Blake was His provision for this leg of my journey.

We became fast friends—a sort of odd couple. He looks like he stepped out of one of those high-fashion magazines. I, on the other hand, do not. He is the picture of grace and style when he runs through Central Park. I suffer from an overactive sweat gland and wear oversize jogging pants. Nevertheless, Blake stuck with me through thick and thin.

"You need to stretch," he admonished me on the first day of our training. "If you don't prepare yourself to run, you could get hurt." Before long, I was twisting and pulling my body in all sorts of directions. I looked like a plump pretzel.

Running was especially difficult for me. My head flopped all over the place, and whenever I hit a hill, I would slow down to a crawl.

"Keep your head down," he said. "Stay focused. And when we hit a hill you need to pick up your speed. Never slow down."

That's easy for you to say. You weigh one hundred thirty pounds.

"And you need to control your breathing," he would say. "You should be able to carry on a conversation when you run."

You've gotta be kidding me. I can barely breathe as it is. And I'm supposed to carry on a conversation?

Sure enough, the next day, Blake demanded that we talk about some obscure theological issue involving predestination.

"Blake, you are my brother in Christ, but if you don't stop talking, I will be predestined to hurt you."

"Runners, on your mark, get set, go!"

And just like that my first 5K road race was underway. The adrenaline rush was amazing as I ran along the first few hundred yards of the course.

Blake was right. Stretching loosened me up. This is going to be fun.

I was surprised at how fast I thought I was moving, until I was passed by an eighty-year-old speed walker wearing purple leg warmers. Do you know how humiliating it is to be passed by an eighty-year-old speed walker wearing purple leg warmers? To make it even worse, he started trash-talking me!

"Be careful," he smirked. "You don't want to break a sweat."

You know, it's a good thing God doesn't smite people still, because I was about ready to order down a heavenly strike.

"Stay focused," Blake would say. "Don't worry about how fast other people are running. You need to run the race you trained for."

I secretly wished the eighty-year-old speed walker would develop a bad case of foot fungus. Nevertheless, I regrouped and continued along my journey—only a mile to go.

Whew! This is a lot harder than I thought.

I wish I could tell you that God revealed all sorts of deep spiritual and theological points along the racecourse. Honestly, I was just concentrating on crossing the finish line without the assistance of an ambulance.

"Who needs water? Stop here for water!"

Every mile or so, they offered refreshment tables—filled with water or Gatorade. We were encouraged to stay hydrated. Even though it was a short race, the warm weather made us susceptible to dehydration.

"Would you like some water, sir?"

"Thanks," I said before stumbling back onto the course. "You don't happen to have any Krispy Kreme doughnuts, do you?"

They did not.

The rest of the race was pretty much a blur. I just remember asking myself how in the world I expected to run a marathon when I could barely finish a 5K race. But first things first, as Blake said. I needed to finish what I had started, and I did—albeit in a dismal time. I ran a fourteen-minute mile. I had been bested by that blasted speed walker—along with nearly the entire field of runners.

As I tumbled across the finish line at the World Financial Center, one of the medics noticed my red hat and came rushing over to see if I required assistance. "Yes," I replied. "I need a nurse and a cheeseburger—and not necessarily in that order."

22

How to Lose Weight Without Spending a Dime

In the beginning, God created the heavens and the earth. He made the cow for cheeseburgers, the chicken for the Baptists, and the pig for barbecuing. And, boy, was it good!

I am a true son of the South. I love my tea sweet, my chicken fried, and my biscuits buttered. But my true passion in life is barbecue. And as we learned in Sunday school, barbecue is pig. It's in the Bible—or so I've heard. If you are hosting a barbecue at your home, there'd better be a piece of pork in the smoker. Burgers and hot dogs do not constitute a barbecue.

If it's not obvious, I love food, and I was a *very* happy fat person. I was watching an episode of *Dr. Phil*. There were all these overweight people onstage, and every last one of them was just as miserable as they could've been. And whenever trouble entered their lives, they stuffed their pieholes with food.

Well, not me. I was one of the happiest fat people in the world. I just loved eating. I loved buttermilk biscuits, fried catfish, my Aunt Norma's broccoli casserole, and my Aunt Sue's Thanksgiving Day turkey. And don't even get me started on Mom's sweet potato pie. I loved chicken-fried steak and chicken-fried chicken. And I loved the holy grail of the food chain: the pig (pork chops, pork rinds, pork and beans). Oh, somebody just say "Amen" and pass the barbecue sauce before I start preaching.

I believe heaven will include the following:

1. A Chick-fil-A franchise
2. Double Chocolate Fudge Coca-Cola Cake from Cracker Barrel
3. A rib joint
4. Paula Deen
5. Butter

Biblical scholars might find fault with the Double Chocolate Fudge Coca-Cola Cake, but you can't convince me the Lord wouldn't have a rib joint somewhere near the pearly gates.

Somewhere along the way, though, I developed a slight problem. I was stuffing so much food into my "temple" there wasn't any room for the Lord. An early indication I was eating a bit much came years ago at a Chinese restaurant in Biloxi, Mississippi. I was on assignment covering a hurricane along with the great Southern Baptist photographer Morris Abernathy. We stopped at an all-you-can-eat Chinese restaurant. After our fourth trip around the buffet, the owner came over to our table, handed us the check and two fortune cookies, and told us, "No more food for you."

When I was a boy, I remember sitting in church and listening to the preacher go on a tear about drinking and gambling and dancing. But there wasn't much talk about gluttony. And in my estimation, anything done in excess is a sin—and that includes overeating.

My cardiologist told me I had a choice to make. I could either keep stuffing my face with Nutter Butters or I could make some changes in my lifestyle and live a long and healthy life. I had been given a second chance, and even someone with my limited brainpower could understand what was at stake.

It wasn't the first time I had tried to lose weight, and that's what worried me. I had tried every program under the sun. But nothing seemed to work for me. So, I decided to pray about it.

> *Lord, I have to be honest. I want to lose this weight. I want to live a healthy life. I want my body to bring honor to You. I don't have the willpower to do this alone. I don't have the discipline to do this. Will You please help me lose this weight? Will You bring people into my life to help me on this journey?*

Friends, my weight-loss campaign started two weeks after I left the hospital, and it hasn't stopped. The Lord not only heard my prayer, but He honored my prayer. It's been downright difficult, but it has been one of the most spiritually rewarding periods in my life.

If you are searching for a quick fix to your weight problem, I'm afraid you are searching in the wrong place. I didn't lose one hundred fifty pounds overnight or in six months. It's been three years since my heart surgery, and I'm still losing weight. The key is to bathe every moment of your life in prayer. Turn your "battle of the bulge" over to the Lord. He will give you the strength you will need to burn away the fat.

So how did I do it? How did I lose one hundred fifty pounds without spending a dime? I did it without Jenny Craig and Richard Simmons. I figured, why pay someone else when I'm the one who has to do all of the work?

So, here's how to do it:

1. *Take personal responsibility for yourself.* Go ahead and fess up. The government did not force you to supersize your quarter-pounder with cheese. Admit to yourself that you are overweight and you want to do something about it.

2. *Build an accountability team.* It might be your spouse or close friends or a minister. Losing weight should be a team sport. I had a great team led by Michael and Blake the Runner. These brothers in Christ kept me from overindulging and kept me focused on the big picture

instead of a plate of doughnuts. It's the eye of the tiger, baby!

3. *Set reasonable goals.* I didn't start off thinking, *Sweet mercy, I've gotta lose one hundred pounds.* Instead, I set small, attainable goals—usually in five-pound increments. And for the first two weeks, I stayed away from the scales. I believe they can be satanic. (And don't be afraid to toss your scales out the window every now and then. You can get them on sale at Wal-Mart.)

4. *Start exercising immediately.* This is important. For the first six months after surgery, the only type of exercise I could do was walking. Well, walking is the best way to lose weight. Grab an iPod, lace up your running shoes, and hit the sidewalk. I'd suggest working yourself up to a mile a day. It's a great way to get your blood pumping and your fat burning. I joined a local running club. It's a great organization that has a passion for helping people stay healthy. I would encourage you to check your local gym or church recreation group for a similar club.

5. *Seek divine guidance.* I believe in the power of prayer. When I first started my weight-loss journey, I asked the Lord to give me the strength and willpower to finish what I was about to start. As much as this has been a physical journey, it's also been a spiritual journey. The Bible says we are supposed to run a good race. It's difficult to do that when we're hauling around excess baggage. And I am walking proof that during my weakest moments, God has been strongest.

The biggest misconception about dieting is what you can and cannot eat. I lost most of my weight eating at my favorite rib joint at least once a week. Yes, it is true. Barbecue can help you lose weight. Just make sure it's the dry-rub type. Just because you are losing weight doesn't mean you need to stop eating good food. It's all about moderation. Let's be sensible. A person can only handle so much cottage cheese. And don't even get me started on celery sticks, unless they come with a side of chicken wings and bleu cheese dressing.

Let's break it down. Your body is like a car. It needs fuel to work. If you fill up your car with cheap gas, there's a pretty good chance you will end up on the back of a tow truck. Likewise, if you constantly stuff your face with too much unhealthy food, your body will not perform at peak performance levels. And if you eat too much chili, there's a good chance your engine might very well backfire!

Now let me give you some very practical (and free) ways to shed some of that excess baggage:

1. *Stay away from restaurants with all-you-can-eat buffets.* There's no earthly reason why you need to eat four pounds of chicken wings at the Sizzler. And for the record, pouring a gallon of ranch dressing on your salad defeats the purpose. You're better off going to McDonald's and supersizing a Big Mac meal. The next time you eat away from home, pick a sit-down restaurant. Skip the appetizer and ask the server if they offer smaller portions.

2. *Stop drinking sugary soft drinks.* My beverage of choice is the Baptist Martini, better known as a Diet Coke. This was a really difficult choice for me. Most Southern kids are nursed on Coca-Cola. I love the original—but, unfortunately, it can really add on the pounds. It's been an acquired taste, but Diet Coke is the way to go, along with organic fruit juices. One of my favorites is cranberry juice. It's heart-healthy. I'm still trying to get my taste buds wrapped around pomegranate juice. Maybe it's just me, but it's hard to drink something that comes off a shrub.

3. *Have a meat-free day.* I know this is heresy, but give it a shot. I eat a lot of vegetables and plenty of salads. It's healthy and filling. Be sensitive with your dressing and skip the cheese and croutons. By the way, whoever came up with the idea of fat-free ranch dressing needs to be deported to Canada. I'm proud to say I've lost all my weight while eating real ranch salad dressing. Your general rule of thumb, of course, is to eat some veggies with your dressing.

4. *Eat a cheeseburger.* Pick a day to splurge. My day is Saturday. I'll typically have a few slices of pizza or a cheeseburger. The key is to enjoy regular food. But I've also made some concessions. Instead of eating fries with my burger, I'll have a salad. Or some days, I'll order a salad with a side order of onion rings.

5. *Avoid elevators.* If you have the opportunity, take the stairs. The added exercise is good for you. Look for ways to add walking to your daily

routine. I usually walk or run at least five miles a day. When you go to the supermarket, park as far from the store as possible. Many schools have running tracks. Drop by after work and walk a few laps. And while you're at it, try doing some stadiums (walking up and down the bleachers). Exercise is fun and it doesn't require bench-pressing a small farm animal.

6. *Get rid of your old clothes*. When I started my weight-loss campaign, I was a size 54 waist. Today, I'm a 36 and getting smaller. Every four waist sizes, I had to buy new pants. Just to make sure the temptation wasn't there, I gave away my old clothes to charity. It's all about total commitment. Never look back.

Losing weight is a long process. Be patient and don't get discouraged. It's just like training for a marathon. You take one step at a time.

23

THE CALL

My father died. And I miss him.

Dad made his own unique mark on this world. He loved. He fought. He married. He raised a family. And now, he's gone.

It all happened so suddenly. His heart began to fail and Mom called me.

"Dad's in the hospital. You need to come to Atlanta."

It's a three-hour flight from New York's LaGuardia Airport to Atlanta. It seemed like a lifetime—staring out that small window, remembering. My earliest memory of Dad is a photograph. It was Christmas Day 1969. I was two years old. Holiday debris was strewn around the den, and Dad was crouching down holding a jack-in-the-box. The photographer captured the blue-and-orange clown in mid-bob, dangling over the side. And there I was—looking fashionable in my white turtleneck and corduroy overalls. I was staring at the strange creature Dad was holding.

But it's what happened just before the photo was snapped that is etched in my memory. I was a timid child. A good gust of wind was enough to send me crying to Mom. So when that clown popped out of the box, I freaked out. I remember lots of screams and tears as I ran through the house looking for a therapist.

But in the photo are Dad and I. It's an image of a father gently reassuring his son, reassuring me, "Everything's going to be okay."

That's what Dad told me when I walked into his hospital room. I was still recovering from my surgery, and I felt a chill as I had flashbacks of my own brush with death. He told me he felt great, but I knew he didn't. He said he wanted to go home, but I knew he wouldn't.

I'm not sure I understood Dad. And, you know, I'm not sure we're supposed to understand our dads. Mine was a paradox. Todd James Starnes Jr. was a blue-collar man, but he used his thick, calloused fingers to play classical guitar. He never got a college education, but he taught himself to read Hebrew and Greek. He was a fighter, but he had a tender heart for the Lord.

Dad was a rough-and-tumble character—the James Dean of Whitehaven High School. He wore a blue-jean jacket over a white T-shirt and played the guitar like it was nobody's business. And, that's how Dad got to hang out with Elvis Presley.

Dad spent his growing-up years running around Memphis with the Smith boys—Elvis' cousins—and, in short order, they formed a band. The cousins lived at Graceland and used to practice behind the house. One day, Elvis showed up while Dad was playing "That's All Right, Momma," an Elvis standard. Afterward, Elvis grinned that Elvis grin and told my daddy, "Jimmy, that's pretty good."

My grandparents, though, weren't all that impressed with Elvis or his gyrating hips. One morning, my grandmother was reading the Memphis newspaper when she saw a photograph of Elvis standing at the front gates of Graceland. On the other side was a gaggle of uncontrollable female fans. But it was the boy standing next to Elvis that caught my grandmother's attention. "Jimmy," she asked, "what are you doing standing next to Elvis Presley?"

Elvis, of course, went on to become a megastar. Dad did not. But he never gave up his dream. Music was the rhythm of his heart, the passion of his life.

Dad came to know Christ in his thirties. A friend invited him to a revival service at the local Baptist church. Dad accepted Jesus that night, and from that day forward our family attended church. Unfortunately, he was never fully able to shake those spiritual demons that plague all of us in this life. His battle with the bottle consumed much of his latter years. In the end, he won the fight, but the damage to his body and to his heart had already been done.

Dad was a dreamer of dreams. Yet, his dreams were always just beyond his grasp. And, sometimes, when I heard him playing his guitar on the front porch of our home, he seemed sad. As if he was on a lifelong journey, searching for meaning, for purpose.

I sat by his side for a week and then had to return to New York. Before I left, he asked me a question.

"Are you happy, son?"

I thought about that question a lot on the plane ride back to New York. In a way, I was my father's son. I had been searching for something in this life, and my dreams always seemed just out of reach. My search uprooted me from the South. It took me to California and ultimately to the Big Apple. I thought about that question, long and hard. And I decided, yes, I was. I was happy.

The call came at three in the morning. I'm not sure why bad news comes at such odd hours. And as much as I was expecting the call, I was still surprised when I heard the voice on the other end.

"Your daddy is gone."

In the end, I believe Dad found what he was looking for. He left me a legacy filled with lessons on triumph and failure, of love lost and love found, and of enduring hope.

He taught me that it's okay to dream dreams. I would like to imagine that Dad is hanging out near the pearly gates playing, "That's All Right, Momma." And Elvis is there saying, "Jimmy, that's pretty good."

My dad died. And I sure do miss him.

24

I HAVE UGLY FEET

I have ugly feet.

I know the Bible talks about beautiful feet, but mine are just plain unattractive. My big toes are abnormally big, the other toes are pudgy, and my feet are flatter than an Iowa cornfield. I don't mean to disparage the appendages the good Lord provided. I'm just a realist.

Thomas, my thirteen-year-old cousin, observed my bare feet on the beach. "Wow," he said. "Look at your feet." Indeed.

Unsightly as they may be, my feet were still functional. Then I was on the final stretch of a six-mile run in Central Park. I turned a corner too quickly and my right foot came down at an unusual angle. I felt a slight sliver of pain shoot around my ankle, but otherwise didn't think much about it.

My good friend Blake the Runner told me to get it checked out. I told him I'd do it after the marathon. He didn't say it, but he gave me that "Don't be a moron" look. And then he told me, "You're crazy." He's probably right.

The following morning, I lumbered out of bed and immediately winced in agony. My foot was about the size of a ripe grapefruit. *That's not good*, I thought. Instead of making a doctor's appointment, I decided to wish the pain away. It didn't work. So five days later, I hobbled over to the emergency room at New York's Methodist Hospital.

I consider myself a fairly ecumenical fellow, but I'd never been to a Methodist hospital before. In Memphis, the Baptists went to the Baptist hospital, the Methodists went to the Methodist hospital, and the atheists went to—well, you can just imagine where they went.

The hospital is not too far from my Brooklyn apartment, and to the best of my knowledge no patients have died in the waiting room while waiting to see a doctor. That actually happened at one of our city's esteemed healing centers.

It took about eight hours to see the doctor and about ten minutes to figure out what was wrong. "It's either broken or it's not," said the doctor. I was in too much pain to offer a pithy retort. A few minutes later I was dispatched to the X-ray department, where I met a technician named Latrice.

"What's your problem, baby?"

"I have an ugly foot," I said matter-of-factly.

She let out a gusty laugh that seemed to shake

162

the room. "Baby, I've heard a lot of problems in my day, but this is a first. Take off that shoe, honey. Let me see what God done give you."

I sat on the edge of the X-ray table, unlaced my running shoes, and pulled out my throbbing foot. Soon, Latrice was ordering me to pose my foot this way and that way, snapping all sorts of shots. There was one particular pose that reminded me of a recent *Vanity Fair* cover. I just needed a bunch of grapes and two anorexic models wearing togas.

"Work it, baby, work it," Latrice said as I flipped and flopped my wounded foot.

After the photo shoot, I was given something to help with the pain. I'm not too sure about the dosage, but I vaguely remember a bizarre moment that involved a physician's assistant and a Bee Gees song. I managed to hit a few high notes on "How Deep Is Your Love." It's been my experience that Bee Gees music sounds much better when you are medicated.

All of that to say I did not have a broken foot—just a bad sprain. My marathon dream had not been dashed after all.

As I was about to leave, I ran into Latrice, the X-ray technician. "I've seen a lot of feet in my day, and baby, your feet got character. You've fine feet."

With a wink she turned to leave, and I hobbled into the dark night, smiling and somewhat amused, humming that Bee Gees song as I waited for a cab.

25

GREATER LOVE HAS NO ONE THAN THIS . . .

I have a hard time telling people I love them. There. I said it.

My friend Sarah said admitting I have a problem is the first step to fixing the problem. But I'm still not sure I really have a problem. I mean, there are just some things guys don't do—like hugging, accessorizing with a man purse, and expressing any shred of emotion.

Whenever I've felt the need to emit emotion, I always ask myself, *What would Chuck Norris do?* It's been said that Chuck Norris cannot love; he can only not kill. That's deep stuff, my friends.

"But you aren't Chuck Norris," Sarah said. "You can't even roundhouse kick." This was true. I was round. And I was as big as a house. But I could not kick.

I'm not sure why the words *I love you* are so difficult for me to say. It's like I have this invisible barrier inside my brain that cuts off any form of emotional attachment. I have a feeling I'm not the only one dealing with this dilemma. Guys are pretty good at masking their true feelings, telling each other "You rock," "You're the man!" or "Who's your daddy?" Okay, scratch that last one. The point is, I explained to Sarah, there are plenty of ways for men to say "I love you" without having to say, "I love you."

"You are in denial, Todd Starnes," Sarah said. "I just don't know why you are making such a big deal about this. You know, one of these days, you're going to wish you'd told someone you love them and it's going to be too late."

It was an unusually quiet day on the fifteenth floor of the Fox News Corner of the World. My desk is in the far right corner of the newsroom with a fantastic view of Forty-seventh Street. And, if I contort my body in just the right position, I can catch a glimpse of the Times Square tower, where they drop the big ball on New Year's Eve.

"Boy, it sure is a quiet news day," said one of our fresh-faced interns. There's an unwritten rule in journalism: Enjoy the quiet days and never, ever say it's a "quiet news day." In mere seconds, a red light flashed on my computer screen and an alarm bell rang. It was breaking news.

Ugh. Just what I needed. I wonder who bombed what this time.

I plopped my feet off my desk, spun around in my chair, and clicked on the blinking red news banner.

URGENT!
DANGEROUS RIP CURRENTS HIT EAST COAST

What's the big deal? I wondered. *Rip currents always hit the coast.* But the rip currents that hit the Jersey shore on July 13, 2008, were far from ordinary. Moments later, a series of alarms rang as another bulletin appeared.

AT LEAST THREE SWIMMERS DEAD— LIFEGUARD IN SOUTH JERSEY MAY BE AMONG FATALITIES

My heart skipped a beat.

Oh, my gosh! That's where Billy works—the Jersey shore.

I grabbed my cell phone and punched in his number. The phone went straight to voice mail. I tried again—no luck, so I sent him a text message.

U OK? CALL ASAP.

I'm sure he's fine. But why didn't he answer his cell phone? Oh, wait. He's at the beach. Of course he wouldn't have his cell phone on. He's working in the lifeguard tower. His phone is probably in his bag . . . I hope.

I stared at my computer screen for what seemed like an eternity, waiting for more details.

The remnants of Hurricane Bertha had turned the Atlantic Ocean into a killing field. Hundreds of swimmers had to be rescued that day—all the while the lifeguards were putting their own lives on the line. And somewhere in all of that chaos was my eighteen-year-old cousin.

My cousin Billy is probably one of the happiest people I know. He's got a perpetual smile and a seemingly endless supply of joy. I'm not sure how he does it because Billy doesn't drink caffeine— although that could explain why he sleeps twelve hours a day.

Aside from family genetics, we share an affinity for beef, scary movies, and Nutter Butters. "I believe Nutter Butters are a blessing from God," he once told me. I agreed.

Last year, Billy called me and announced his intention to become an honest-to-goodness lifeguard. I can't think of a better summertime job for a teenage boy—hanging out on the beach all day, rescuing beautiful women and administering CPR to them. Billy certainly had the credentials. He swam like a fish and held a school record on his swim team. But Billy is also a skinny fellow—really skinny.

He told me one day, "I just got my body fat checked. It's 3 percent. What's yours?"

I told him if he ever asked that question again, I'd delete him from my will.

I wondered, though, if he was physically up for the grueling work of being a lifeguard. Well, what Billy lacked in body mass, he made up for in sheer grit and determination. And would you believe that my one-hundred-fifteen-pound cousin made the lifeguard squad? "I can do all things through Christ who strengthens me" (Phil. 4:13).

Billy soon discovered, though, that being a lifeguard was not quite like *Baywatch*. "For one thing," he said, "all the beautiful people know how to swim." I never really thought of it like that. For every Jessica Simpson pulled from the water, some poor lifeguard has to perform mouth-to-mouth on a Rosie O'Donnell.

As I waited for my cell phone to ring, I remembered the immense measure of pride I felt as I watched him one day on duty at the lifeguard stand. Here was a young man who answered God's call on his life to serve others. Billy willingly put his own life at risk to save others. What kind of a person would do something like that?

The Bible tells about such a person: "Greater love has no one than this, than to lay down one's life for his friends" (John 15:13). I have been blessed and encouraged by Billy's gentle spirit and his kind heart. He is growing into a strong man of God. And I'm most blessed to know that he is not only my cousin, but we are brothers in the Lord.

I was about to rent a car and drive to Atlantic City when my cell phone rang.

"Todd, it's Billy."

"Are you okay? We've been following the news reports. . . ."

"Oh, geez. I'm fine."

After a few minutes of idle chatter, I was about to hang up the phone when I remembered Sarah's admonition about sharing my feelings.

"Hey, Bill?"

"Yeah?"

I stuttered and stammered as I tried to cough up those three very difficult words.

"Well, I uh, just want you to know I uh . . ."

"Yeah?"

Boy, this really is hard. I took a deep breath, swallowed hard, and just blurted it out.

"You're awesome, man!"

And then we said goodbye.

Gimme a break, folks. I'm taking baby steps here.

26

Mom and the First Lady

A buzz rippled across the pews at the First Baptist Church. The pastor announced that the following Sunday President and Mrs. Carter would be coming to town. They would not only be attending the morning worship service, but Mr. Jimmy and Miss Rosalynn would also join the congregation for their annual dinner-on-the-grounds. Mom could hardly contain herself.

Imagine, she thought, *preparing a meal for the former president of the United States!* Dad was not all that impressed. President Carter *was* a Democrat, he reminded Mom. But when it came to home cooking, Kathy Starnes was bipartisan. She firmly believed that world peace could be achieved through a dinner table piled high with ham, country-fried steak, buttermilk biscuits, butter beans, sweet potato pie, and a few gallons of sweet tea.

171

Mom left church that afternoon with a newfound sense of purpose—sort of like a Paula Deen on crack. She was determined to prepare a dish that would change the course of history—a dish that a future generation would define as the turning point in American politics. The dish she selected was potato salad.

Mom ordered Dad to the supermarket with a list of ingredients. Only the finest would do—potatoes, onions, celery, mayonnaise, a variety of spices, and her secret ingredient: a dash of mustard. She started off the week making practice batches, working night and day, much to the chagrin of my father, who did not care for potato salad.

By Thursday, Mom was getting exasperated. The potato salad was either too lumpy or too mushy. She tossed aside her apron and huffed out of the kitchen. "I only have seven days to get this right," she complained. Dad wasn't very helpful. "I don't see what the big deal is," he said. "It only took God six days to make the world." Fortunately, Mom didn't have a cast-iron skillet handy.

Mom called her prayer circle for a bit of divine intervention, and it must have worked. On Sunday morning, she produced a potato salad worthy of a former peanut farmer turned president.

There's nothing quite like a Sunday afternoon dinner-on-the-grounds—especially for Southern Baptists. Here's how it works: After the Sunday sermon, the congregation is dismissed to the fellowship hall, where tables are piled high with all sorts of homemade goodness—fresh fried chicken, country ham, congealed salads, biscuits, greens, and more pies than you can shake a stick at. Everything, and I do mean everything, is made from scratch. Why, showing up at a Baptist church with a bucket of KFC might just get you kicked off the membership roll, and it would certainly put you on somebody's prayer list.

The preacher that day was particularly long-winded. He took us to the lake of fire and to the pearly gates, tossing in some hellfire and brimstone for good measure. And after singing all five verses of the invitation hymn, the congregation had worked up quite an appetite.

Mr. Jimmy and Miss Rosalynn dutifully got in line and began loading up their plates. And, sure enough, both managed to find room for some of Mom's potato salad. A while later, Miss Rosalyn came over to meet Mom, and with a flourish of grace she pronounced the potato salad absolutely delicious.

Well, praise the Lord! Dad was relieved, I was astonished, and Mom was on cloud nine. First lady Rosalynn Carter loved her potato salad. And Mom was a registered Republican!

It seemed like such an insignificant moment in life, but to my mother that compliment meant the world. Many years later and many miles away from Georgia, I would come to understand why.

The telephone call came shortly before I delivered the evening newscast. The voice on the other end sounded distant and void of emotion. He identified himself as a police officer. "It is my duty to inform you...." I asked him to stop—somehow hoping that if he did not recite his message it wouldn't be true. But it was. Mom was gone. After sixty-one years, her heart simply ran out of seasons.

Mom had been in frail health for years, but after Dad passed she seemed to lose the will to live. Her doctor told me it wouldn't be long, and sadly, she was right. For the last six months of her life, Mom was confined to a bed, hooked up to a ventilator. I sat by her side, combed her hair, read her stories, and told her about my marathon training. We worked out a rudimentary system of communication involving finger taps and sign language. And then, one day, she just died.

During her funeral, the preacher asked for people to share something special about Mom. The piano player went first. She said it might seem odd, but she would always remember Mom's sweet potato pie. Then, somebody else chimed in about her corn-bread dressing. There were a few nods, and a few amens. Aunt Lynn got teary-eyed when she talked about Mom's corn-bread dressing. And then, I remembered that day a long time ago at the First Baptist Church as Mom beamed with pride at her presidential potato salad.

I've thought a lot about my mother's life. She could've done whatever she wanted. She was a gifted and beautiful singer. But she chose to make her life at home. She was a housewife, and the kitchen was her kingdom. She never achieved fame or fortune. Instead, she found joy in cooking a good meal and found satisfaction in the full bellies and empty plates at her table. And she will always be remembered for the way she used her culinary gifts to serve up heaping helpings of love, piled high with sugary sweetness, and a dollop of buttery goodness on top.

27

WOBBLY KNEES AND NERVES

A number had been rattling around inside my head—502. That's the number of people who had started last year's New York City Marathon and never made it across the finish line. All those weeks and months of blood, sweat, and tears—and, for one reason or another, their dreams were dashed.

I didn't want to be one of those people.

To be honest, I had a hard time sleeping that week. I was plumb tuckered out! The marathon was just a few days away, and I was beginning to wonder if I was really going to have what it took to make it across the finish line. Did I run as often as I should have? Did I lose enough weight? Did I buy the right running shoes? Crazy stuff, honestly.

But I had really been anxious about my knees, specifically my left knee. It started aching just after I hurt my foot.

I really appreciate my knees, even if I don't show it. For the past ten years, they've been hauling around three hundred pounds of excess baggage. It's a good thing knees can't talk. If so, mine would probably give me an earful. "What in the world is he doing to us? A marathon? Good grief, give it a rest!"

It rained on Sunday. It was a pretty miserable day with dark, gloomy skies and a cold, steady rain. Probably not the best running weather, but I ran anyway. Central Park was virtually empty—just a few other hardy souls and me, plodding along with my iPod, wiping the rain from my glasses. I ran alongside the Metropolitan Museum of Art, up around the reservoir, and bolted up through the North Woods. I hit a spread of loose gravel, and that's when it happened. I felt that pain again. *Stupid knee.*

I stopped for a moment and caught my breath, remembering the warning my heart surgeon delivered. "We can vouch for the new heart valve holding up, but your knees are a different story." *Stupid knee.*

The pain subsided and I was feeling better, but I had a really bad case of prerace jitters. I'd heard rumors that somebody was starting up an office pool. *If that's the case, I might need to hedge my bet!*

A few days later I was moping around the Fox News Corner of the World, and you'll never guess who showed up in our fifteenth-floor newsroom—Frank Shorter! *The Frank Shorter.* The guy who brought home the Olympic gold medal in the marathon in 1972! And he also has a gold medal in making folks feel like a million dollars.

"I'm very envious of you," he said.

Well, butter my biscuit! I couldn't believe it—
Frank Shorter envious of me?

"Your first marathon is always the most exciting. You have the most trepidation going in, but
I think it's also the most satisfying when you get
done because you realize you were really able to
do it and achieve the goals."

"You're the same kind of athlete as the person
up in the front of the pack," he added. "You are
running the same distance. You are expending
the same amount of energy."

But Frank did not pull any punches. He told
me to gird myself for what was going to be the
most difficult adventure I'd ever attempted. He
assured me that once I got to the twenty-mile
mark, it was going to get nasty. "You will need to
use every mental trick you can to get yourself to
the finish," he told me.

I really appreciated his honest assessment
of my predicament. He said he believed in
me, and—you know something?—deep down
I believed in myself. I was going to have sore
knees, and I'd be aching in parts of my body
that I didn't even know I had. But that's what
happens when you push your body and your
mind to the limit.

There's a spiritual lesson here.

> For as the body is one and has many mem-
> bers, but all the members of that one body,
> being many, are one body, so also is Christ.
> For by one Spirit we were all baptized

into one body—whether Jews or Greeks, whether slaves or free—and have all been made to drink into one Spirit. For in fact the body is not one member but many. If the foot should say, "Because I am not a hand, I am not of the body," is it therefore not of the body? And if the ear should say, "Because I am not an eye, I am not of the body," is it therefore not of the body? If the whole body were an eye, where would be the hearing? If the whole were hearing, where would be the smelling? But now God has set the members, each one of them, in the body just as He pleased. And if they were all one member, where would the body be? (1 Cor. 12:12-19).

The apostle Paul continues to exhort believers in 1 Corinthians 12 by telling us, in verse 26, "And if one member suffers, all the members suffer with it; or if one member is honored, all the members rejoice with it."

My preparation for the marathon had been a team effort. It started back in Sacramento with Jeannine and Tom and Wayne and Nancy. It continued in New York with Billy and Blake. If I finished the race, we would rejoice together. If I failed, we would suffer together. Each person in my team brought a distinct gift to the table—Billy, with his gentle and encouraging spirit; Blake, with his determination and can-do attitude; Jeannine, with her prophetic voice; my grandmother, with her daily dosage of common sense; and my family of prayer warriors.

180

We were the body—the team. And they would be my support on marathon day.

This Old Testament passage came to my mind one day when I was in the North Woods: *It is God who arms me with strength, and makes my way perfect. He makes my feet like the feet of deer, and sets me on my high places* (Ps. 18:32-33).

That would be my prayer on marathon day— that He would take me to the high places, wobbly knees, nerves, and all.

181

28

RUNNING A GOOD RACE

The New York City Marathon is one of the greatest road races in the world. More than thirty-seven thousand runners would attempt to complete the 26.2-mile course through all five of the city's boroughs. The race starts in Staten Island and winds its way through Brooklyn, Queens, and the Bronx before ending in Central Park.

The field of runners included professionals racing for a paycheck and amateurs like me running for the glory of crossing the finish line of a marathon. But we all had one thing in common: we all had a story.

The marathon is the Mount Everest of running. And the New York City Marathon is a tough race. It would challenge me physically and mentally. I'd been training for more than six months—running five miles a day through ice, snow, rain, humidity, and scorching heat.

I'd run more than a dozen races since my heart surgery. I'd finished four-milers, 10Ks, and two half-marathons. I'd spent weeks in the gym, building muscle and endurance. But even with all that training, I was still about thirty pounds overweight and I was worried about how that might impact my ability to finish the race.

When I had the opportunity to meet Frank Shorter, he said, "Have some fun out there. Just remember—it's not how fast you run the race; it's how you finish."

Isn't that how God intends for us to live life? It's not necessarily about how successful we are. It's not about coming in first. It's about living the life God wants us to live. It's about trusting Him for the strength we need to get through the good days and the bad.

Over the course of my life, I developed a bad habit—I would begin a task, but sometimes I failed to finish what I had started. That was my greatest fear as I stood at the starting line of the marathon.

Lord, I'm not sure if I can do this. Please give me the strength to run this race.

My day had started at three in the morning. I woke up, showered, and put on several layers of clothes. It was early November, and in New York City that meant it was chilly. The race organizers recommended we wear layers, and as the race progressed we could shed our clothes by the side of the road. It was common to find piles of sweatshirts and outerwear dumped along the raceway.

I took the subway to South Ferry in lower Manhattan and boarded the Staten Island Ferry, where buses then shuttled us to the starting line. We were passing by the Statue of Liberty when Uncle Jerry from Coldwater, Mississippi, called to wish me luck.

"Be sure to keep it between the ditches, and don't embarrass the family," he said.

A production team from Fox News Channel had been documenting my journey for the past few months, and I had been writing a daily blog on *www.Foxnewsradio.com*. I was surprised by the amount of email I received from readers and the words of encouragement they offered. I gleaned a certain amount of courage from their profiles in courage.

I was particularly touched by a letter I received from one of our soldiers who had just returned from fighting in Iraq. His name was James, and he was a master sergeant in the Marines. He was a poster child for the Marines—a buff, sturdy soldier, a man's man. He played football, ran marathons, and was an athletic specimen. But during a routine checkup, his doctor discovered a problem with his heart. His aortic valve was beginning to fail, and he needed to have open-heart surgery.

As James recounted in his letter, he was distraught. He went home and began searching the

Internet for information about aortic-valve surgery. And that's how he found out about my blog.

"I need you to tell me if I'll ever be able to throw the football with my son," he wrote.

Over the days leading up to his surgery, we traded a number of emails and I assured him that he would be there for his son. He would be able to lead a healthy life. Sure enough, James came through his surgery just fine. And one day, he will be able to toss around a football with his boy.

And today, I would be running this race for people like James—a fellow survivor.

I was running the New York City Marathon for 26.2 reasons—thanks to then Governor Mike Huckabee. To borrow a phrase from Sean Hannity, I believe Mike Huckabee is a great American. Anybody who wants to name Chuck Norris as our secretary of defense has my vote!

I met the governor about a year before he ran for the Republican presidential nomination. Our stories were quite similar. We were both Southern Baptists, we were both overweight, and we had both lost a tremendous amount of weight. He ran the New York City Marathon in 2006, and I had a chance to interview him for Fox News Radio.

"This is going to be one of the hardest things you will ever do in your life," he said. The governor suggested I dedicate each mile to a person who has made an impact on my life—someone who offered a helping hand along my journey.

"And those last 0.2 miles," he said, "that's the part of the race you run for yourself."

"It is God who arms me with strength, and makes my way perfect. He makes my feet like the feet of deer, and sets me on my high places" (Ps. 18:32-33).

I recited that passage of Scripture from the Old Testament as thousands of us were herded into our starting blocks. This was it—the moment I'd been preparing for. I was about to run a marathon. My cardiologist was right—I really was nuts!

"Runners, on your mark, get set, go!"

And just like that, my race to the finish line started. The course started uphill over the Verrazano-Narrows Bridge. It links Staten Island to Brooklyn and offers a stunning view of the Statue of Liberty and lower Manhattan. I listened to Faith Hill's a cappella rendition of "Amazing Grace" as I trotted across the bridge. Billy had helped me program one of the quirkiest marathon mixes in musical history. Throughout the day, I would be listening to everything from the Brooklyn Tabernacle Choir and Steven Curtis Chapman to the All-American Rejects and Barry Manilow.

I was especially surprised by the crowds. Around two million spectators lined the course. Many of us had written our names on our shirts, and strangers would shout out words of encouragement to us.

"Way to go, Todd!"

"Looking good, baby!"

"You can run fast for a fat boy!"

That last shout came from some guy in the Bronx.

And, there were dozens of bands playing live music—from rock and roll to jazz. A few churches had their entire choirs performing worship music for us. It was a uniquely New York experience. Total strangers offered us encouragement. And then there was the guy in Brooklyn who was handing out free cartons of cigarettes.

My fellow runners were an interesting bunch. Some were dressed in costumes like Batman and Robin. Another guy dressed like Papa Smurf, and two fellows ran as The Blues Brothers. One runner tore past me at breakneck speed dressed up as a matador. I glanced behind me to make sure there wasn't a bull coming up from the rear.

I was well into Brooklyn when I realized I was moving along at a pretty good clip—too good, actually. Billy and Blake warned me about my pace. I hit the 5K mark and realized I was running about a nine-minute mile.

Holy cow! That's way too fast.

I was supposed to be running an eleven-minute mile. There was no way I was going to be able to keep up that pace. I needed to slow down—and fast. By mile seven, I was forced to slow down when I felt a slight gurgle.

That doesn't feel quite right.

All I had for dinner the night before was pasta— and I was about to have it again. Fortunately, there were plenty of bathrooms along the course, and I made it to one just before I lost my cookies. The number of port-a-potties had apparently been an issue in past marathons. Prior to the race, they made general announcements to the runners instructing them about rules for the road.

"Attention runners: anyone caught using the bathroom on the racecourse will be disqualified."

Never in a million years would I have imagined that using the bathroom on the side of the road would be an issue. I mean, really! Would people actually drop their drawers and do their business right in front of God and country? On second thought, this *is* New York City. It's bad enough that we had to dodge potholes, but now we had to be on the lookout for people's dingle berries? Sweet mercy!

My pit stop set me back about ten minutes. I was a bit off-kilter, but I was on my way, when suddenly I felt a slight pain in my foot.

What in the world is going on? I feel like my warranty just expired.

The pain was so severe I decided to pull into a medical station around mile ten. A doctor pulled off my shoe and peeled off my sock.

He let out a whistle. "Wow. Check out the size of that blister! I've never seen one that big."

I peered down and my eyes bugged out.

Sweet mercy!

"Well, we have two options here. You can either pull out of the race or we can pop that thing, slap some ointment on it, and send you on your way."

I told him to pop that sucker so I could get back in the race. Before I left, the doctor took a large tongue depressor, dipped it into a gallon jug of petroleum jelly, and ordered me to lift my leg.

"Excuse me?" I said, slightly bewildered.

"It's just petroleum jelly," he said. "We should lubricate your thigh. It will help cut down on chafing."

I politely declined. I had already thrown up and had a blister popped. I wasn't about to let a guy slather my thigh with petroleum jelly on national television. I wanted to maintain at least some shred of dignity.

I was beginning to show signs of fatigue, and I had only run ten miles. I wasn't expecting to tire out so quickly. Maybe, I thought, it was just a phase.

I can do this. I've been training for months for this. I've invested too much in this race to stop.

And then I thought about Billy and the family waiting for me farther down the racecourse. There was no way I could let them down. I just could not let that happen.

Lord, You wanted me to run this race. I've done everything I can do. Please don't let me fail.

I was in trouble and I hadn't even reached the dangerous part of the race—mile eighteen, when even the most experienced runners hit the wall.

29

A Gentle Breeze

I was somewhere in Queens when I hit the wall. One minute I was plodding along, and the next I was barely able to move. It was as if someone had turned my legs into putty. Professional runners call it "hitting the wall."

It's actually a physical condition that afflicts every marathon runner. Our bodies are fueled by carbohydrates, which are in turn converted into something called glycogen. The glycogen burns quickly to provide us with quick energy. But there's a catch. Our bodies can only store enough glycogen for about eighteen to twenty miles of running. And when the glycogen runs low, the body must burn fat for energy. Fat doesn't burn as easily, and that leads to dramatic fatigue.

I pulled into one of the refueling stations along the course and asked for some help. "I've hit the wall," I said. "I need a six-pack of glycogen to go." The medics laughed and explained it wasn't quite that simple.

"You need to eat something," said a marathon physician. "We need to get some carbs into your body—cookies, candy, something like that."

"Got any Nutter Butters?" I asked, as sweat poured down my face.

"No Nutter Butters," he replied.

"How about a cheeseburger?"

"Sir," he replied, "you are running a marathon. You can't eat a cheeseburger in the middle of a marathon. It would be like popping popcorn on a trampoline."

The conversation lasted maybe forty-five seconds as they plopped two liquid gel packs into my hands and ordered me to swallow the contents and keep moving. I'm not quite sure what was in that stuff, but it had the consistency of chocolate-covered grits.

"You can't stop," the medic told me. "You must keep running. You've come too far to quit. This is gut-check time. You've got to will yourself across the finish line."

My mind wanted to keep running, but my body wasn't sold on the plan. I was about eighteen miles into the marathon. I had family and friends waiting for me at the finish line, and I wasn't quite sure I could make it.

As I made the approach to the Queensboro Bridge, I thought for certain I would collapse. My run had been reduced to a slight jog, and the approach to the bridge was about a half-mile incline. I was in such pain—emotionally and physically. I literally slammed into the wall. My foot was throbbing, my clothes were soaked, and I was drenched in sweat and dirt.

All of my planning, all of my training, and this was it. I had failed. I had failed my family, my friends, and myself. I was despondent. I would've yelled if I'd had the strength. Instead, I prayed a simple prayer: *Lord, I can't do this without Your help.*

There's an amazing story in the Old Testament. The prophet Elijah had been chased from the land. That powerful prophet of God had been reduced to hiding in a cave. One day the Lord God told Elijah to go and stand on the mountain.

> And behold, the Lord passed by, and a great and strong wind tore into the mountains and broke the rocks in pieces before the Lord, but the Lord was not in the wind; and after the wind an earthquake, but the Lord was not in the earthquake; and after the earthquake a fire, but the Lord was not in the fire; and after the fire a still small voice. So it was, when Elijah heard it, that he wrapped his face in his mantle and went out and stood in the entrance of the cave. Suddenly a voice came to him, and said, "What are you doing here, Elijah?" (1 Kings 19:11-13).

And, during the New York City Marathon, the voice of God came to me as I stood on the Queensboro Bridge.

193

"What are you doing here, Todd?"

At first I thought I was having a medical condition. I'm a Baptist. Typically, God doesn't call audibles with my denomination. And in my current physical condition, I was almost convinced I was having some sort of breakdown. But the voice persisted.

"What are you doing here, Todd?"

What *was* I doing there? Was I there for my own glory? Was I there to please my family? Honestly, I was. I was so consumed with bouts of "me-itis" that I had lost focus of the true prize — the glory of Christ. It was His calling, after all, not mine, that put me in this race. I was supposed to be running for God's glory, not mine. The Lord had sidelined me in the middle of the race to remind me why I was in the race.

My spiritual batteries had been recharged, but my physical batteries were drained. *How in the world am I supposed to finish the race?* I wondered. And then I remembered something Billy had told me.

"Just put one foot in front of the other," he said. "It's all about pace — your pace. If you go out too hard, you'll die out too quickly. You can do it, Todd. I'm praying for you."

I remembered a passage of Scripture that I had shared with Billy a few months before the marathon: "I can do all things through Christ who strengthens me" (Phil. 4:13). Christ can give us the strength to face adversity — even self-inflicted adversities like running marathons. I had done all I could do. I was maxed out. The last 8.2 miles were definitely going to need a God-sized miracle. As I crossed over the East River, I felt a gentle gust of wind brush against my face and I felt refreshed, much like Elijah must have felt that day long ago when he encountered the King of kings on the mountaintop.

Thank You, Lord.

I smiled, wiped the sweat and grit off my face, took a deep breath, and put one foot in the front of the other—first a walk, then a jog, and by the time I reached the end of the bridge, I was back in the race.

30

FINISHING WHAT I STARTED

When I started this journey, I had two goals: finish the marathon, and stay alive. And I was determined to run across the finish line. There wasn't any way I would let Billy or Blake see me walking. This was the moment that I had to put it all out there. This was the moment that I had to finish what I had started. Somewhere along Fifth Avenue in Harlem, I was beginning to have serious reservations about whether I could follow through with my goals.

My knees were throbbing and my sore foot was so swollen it was pushing out the sides of my shoe. I still had more than two miles to go.

Maybe death wouldn't be such a bad way to go out. Perhaps I could just pick out a nice tree in Central Park and sprawl out under the branches. "Here lies Todd. He tried to run the New York City Marathon, but he failed."

I remembered what Frank Shorter told me a few days earlier. "You have to go into this race with your eyes wide open," he said. "Don't worry about how fast you run. And be sure to have a whole series of backup plans. Run. Walk. Stop. The pleasing part of the marathon is finishing the distance, and that is the biggest challenge—the distance."

I had to will myself to keep going, to keep pushing my body. Other runners were beginning to slow down, too, and some actually started walking. Not me. I couldn't do that. I promised myself and my family that I was going to run the race. There was no room for debate.

You can do it, Todd. I'm praying for you.

That was the text of an email Billy sent me earlier in the day. He reminded me to put the All-American Rejects song "Move Along" in my marathon mix. I was more than a mile from the finish line when the song pounded through my earphones.

That's it, I thought. *I've got to keep moving—just keep moving.* Forget the twenty-five miles I had already run. This was a 1.2-mile road race. The cheering grew louder as I picked up my pace. I turned and told another runner, "I don't know about you, but I'm not going to let this race beat me." I remembered Blake's instructions to keep my head down, pump my arms, and step on the gas when I hit the hills. It seemed like hours, but it was only minutes, as the course veered back into Central Park near the reservoir and followed a path I had run every day for the past six months.

This was the mile I dedicated to my family, and I'm so glad I did. Without their inspiration I would never have made it out of the starting gate. I ignored the pain and the agony and pressed on toward the prize.

And then, I hit the 0.2-mile mark, the last leg of the race, the race that Governor Huckabee told me to run for myself. I had programmed the "Hallelujah Chorus" into my iPod. I felt like it was more than appropriate. My participation in this race was nothing short of a miracle.

The final stretch took me along Central Park Drive South, where thousands of people were waving banners and cheering. My face felt flush as I tried my best to look like the professional runner that I was not.

The course shifted to the right at Columbus Circle as we raced down a hill back into Central Park. The finish line was in sight. I could see the finish line. I was exhausted, filthy, and filled with adrenaline. Every step I made seemed to be in slow motion. I could hear Uncle Bill, Jen, Blake, and Billy cheering my name, but I did not take my eye off the prize.

It had taken three years of planning and training, but I was about to cross the finish line of the 2007 New York City Marathon. It wasn't exactly a photo finish. I was beaten by a guy with one leg and two Italians smoking cigarettes.

My time won't make the record books—six hours and fifty-three minutes—but it was my time. The overweight guy with a mechanical heart valve had finished what he had started. I had completed the 26.2 miles of the New York City Marathon. I ran a good race. I kept my eye on the prize, and as a stranger placed a medal around my neck, I began to cry. A sense of accomplishment overwhelmed me as I realized that this chapter in my life was coming to a close.

God had taken the "least of these" and had allowed me to run a marathon, to step out of my comfort zone, to step out in faith. And I had followed His call.

The cheering subsided. I embraced my family for an emotional reunion. And then, it was over.

"What are you going to do now?" Billy asked.

"Well, I don't know about you guys, but I'm ready for some barbecue."

31

LIVE LIKE YOU WERE LIVING

I love country music. It's the kind of music that makes America the greatest country on the planet. A country song just tells it like it is—plain and simple. It's music that speaks to my soul.

Folks like Johnny Cash, Dolly, and Hank know how to sing a song that'll make even the burliest truck driver cry like a newborn baby. Even the worst country music songs are still better than some of the stuff on today's pop charts (paging Kevin Federline).

Honestly, who among us can forget these classics?

1. If You Can't Live Without Me, Then Why Aren't You Dead?
2. Get Off the Stove, Grandma, You're Too Old to Ride the Range
3. Jesus Loves Me, But He Can't Stand You

4. I Wouldn't Take Her to a Dogfight,
   'Cause I'm Afraid She'd Win
5. You're the Reason Our Kids Are Ugly

As my Uncle Jerry from Coldwater, Mississippi, says, "If those songs don't put a teardrop in your eye, then something's just not right with you."

A lot of folks have asked me why I did it. "Why did you run the New York City Marathon? Was it really worth the risk? Why would you do something so dangerous? Are you nuts?"

Tim McGraw sings a song about a man who has only a short time to live. I heard that song just before I went into the hospital, and the lyrics had a profound impact on my journey.

As the seconds on the clock ticked away, I was flooded with images of missed opportunities and wasted moments. I was reminded of opportunities I failed to take. Don't get me wrong, I've had a wonderful life, but there are some things that I sure would've done differently. Strangely, it was a pretty long list. Big things, like never getting married; and little things, like never watching the sun set over the Golden Gate Bridge. I thought about all of those moments as I listened to Tim McGraw croon his song that tells of the things the man has done since learning of his imminent death.

I don't believe the Lord calls us to live a timid life. I think that's why stepping out in faith is so difficult. It's risky. There are no guarantees, only blind and absolute trust that Christ will lead, but only if we follow. So I decided that if I survived the heart surgery, I would lead a very different life—one that was unapologetically on fire for Christ.

I made a list of things I'd like to do before I cross over into glory. There are big things and not-so-big things, and some silly things on my list. Here's a sampling:

1. Get married. (Working on it.)
2. Do the Hustle. (Did it.)
3. Ride a bike across the Golden Gate Bridge. (Did it.)
4. Go surfing in the Pacific Ocean. (Did it.)
5. Retire. (In this economy?)
6. Spend more time with family. (Doing it.)
7. Take long walks on nice days. (Did it.)
8. Go singing in the rain. (Did that, too.)
9. Become a vegetarian. (Just kidding. Really.)
10. Memorize more Scripture. (Doing it.)

How about yourself? Do you have a list? Are there some things that you'd like to do but never really got around to doing? What about your secret passions and dreams? There are 525,600 minutes in a year, folks. So open up your laptop, your Black-Berry, or grab a piece of paper, and write down some things you'd like to do this year. And then—do them!

It's that simple. Really.

I may never go skydiving or ride a bull, but I have survived open-heart surgery. I've lost a lot of weight, and I've run the New York City Marathon.

And somewhere along the way, I learned that God's mercies are new every morning and that His strength is perfect when mine is not. And, with apologies to Tim McGraw, I've chosen to live the rest of my days not like I was dying. Instead, I've chosen to live like I was living.

EPILOGUE

Time passes, seasons fade, but the love of the Lord lasts forever. It's been three years since I was given a new lease on life, and the good days far outnumber the bad. My heart valve is still clicking on all cylinders. I just went in for my three-thousand-mile lube job and was given a clean bill of health along with a wash and wax (which I declined).

I'm still losing weight, and I'm still running five miles a day through rain, sleet, snow, hail, and a taxi strike. And I've started training for my first triathlon. My cardiologist thinks I'm nuts, but he signed off on the paperwork.

"I can vouch for the heart valve, but not your knees."

Billy promised to help me with the swimming leg of the competition, and Blake said he would handle the running part of it. I'm still searching for a cycling coach. I wonder what Lance Armstrong is up to these days?

I'm excited about the triathlon, but there's a caveat. I'm only going to do it if I can reach my target weight of one hundred forty pounds. Unlike the marathon, where you can wear anything you want, the triathlon has a strict dress code. Every competitor is required to wear a formfitting bodysuit. And I mean really form-fitting—something that makes Britney Spears look like a prude.

Trust me; those getups reveal every nook and cranny you have. I would need to rub myself with about a pound of butter to squeeze into one of those things. Since I don't have the physique of Michael Phelps, I've decided to spare the nation and my family the shame of what would've become an instant hit on YouTube. But my day will come, and if you see some pasty white guy floating past the Statue of Liberty, you might want to throw me a life preserver.

The other day I was at the Fox News Corner of the World when one of my colleagues pulled me into an empty studio.

"How do you do it?"

"How do I do what?"

"All the stuff you've been through—your surgery, your parents. How come you aren't on top of a roof somewhere? Why are you so happy?"

I thought about it for a moment and smiled as I remembered an old hymn we used to sing in church.

> I sing because I'm happy,
> I sing because I'm free,
> For His eye is on the sparrow,
> And I know He watches me.

The only reason I survived these past three years is because of my relationship with Jesus Christ.

I made a decision to follow Jesus when I was thirteen years old. I came to an understanding that getting baptized was not enough. Going to church was not enough. Going to Sunday school was not enough. To truly have an eternal relationship with Christ meant to admit that I was a sinner, to ask forgiveness, and to invite Jesus to enter my heart. It was a choice I made—to surrender my life to Him.

Do you have a relationship with Jesus? Do you know where you will spend eternity? If not, I encourage you to consider a relationship with Jesus Christ.

"For God so loved the world that He gave His only begotten Son, that whoever believes in Him should not perish but have everlasting life" (John 3:16).

Looking back over this leg of my journey, I don't believe I could've made it without my relationship with Christ. He sustained me through some really lousy days, and He carried me through the really bad days. Do you remember the Steven Curtis Chapman hit "His Strength Is Perfect When Our Strength Is Gone"? There's a lot of spiritual truth in that song. My strength has been depleted more times than I care to remember.

This journey has been hard—really hard. Some days I didn't even want to get out of bed. But, at just the right moment, I would get an email or my phone would ring and someone would offer me a word of encouragement. I came to understand that God's mercies are truly tender and they are new every morning.

I'm not sure why things turned out the way they did for me. I don't have a clue. I know that it's part of God's master plan for my life, but honestly, I don't know where I'm going next week, much less next year. But I do know this: we are called as His children to believe, step out in faith, and trust that God will guide our path.

We accumulate many titles along life's journey. Some are called fathers. Others are called sons. Some are called friends. Still others are called brothers. As I reflect on these many months, I believe I now can add a new title to my name— survivor.

Now, if you'll excuse me, I'm ready to eat some ribs.